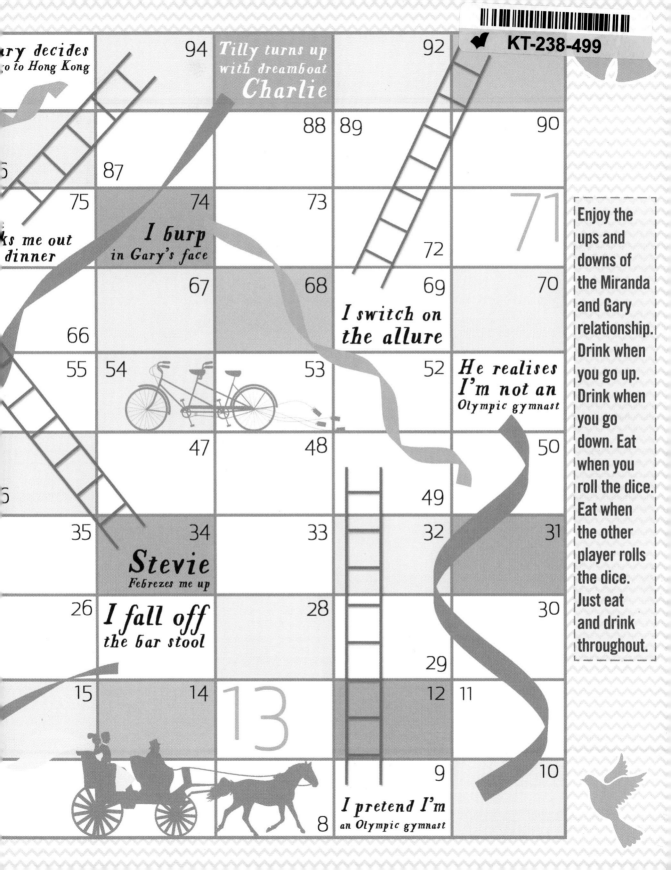

ry decides
to Hong Kong 94

Tilly turns up
with dreamboat
Charlie 92

88 89 90

87

75 74 73 71

72

ks me out
dinner *I burp*
in Gary's face

67 68 *I switch on
the allure* 69 70

66

55 54 53 52 *He realises
I'm not an*
Olympic gymnast

47 48 50

49

35 34 33 32 31

Stevie
Febrezes me up

26 *I fall off*
the bar stool 28 30

29

15 14 13 12 11

9 10

8 *I pretend I'm*
an Olympic gymnast

Enjoy the ups and downs of the Miranda and Gary relationship. Drink when you go up. Drink when you go down. Eat when you roll the dice. Eat when the other player rolls the dice. Just eat and drink throughout.

The Best of Miranda

The Best of Miranda

Favourite episodes
plus added treats - such fun!

Miranda Hart

HODDER &
STOUGHTON

First published in Great Britain in 2014 by
Hodder & Stoughton

An Hachette UK company

1

Copyright © KingMaker Productions Ltd, 2014

Extra funny bits by Jiksaw Ltd, 2014

The copyright in the stills and images from the BBC
'Miranda' series is owned by the BBC

A CIP catalogue record for this title is available from the British Library

Hardback ISBN 978 1 444 79934 7
Trade Paperback ISBN 978 1 444 79935 4
Ebook ISBN 978 1 444 79936 1

Printed and bound in Italy by L.E.G.O. Spa

Designed by Janette Revill

Hodder & Stoughton policy is to use papers that are natural, renewable
and recyclable products and made from wood grown in sustainable forests.
The logging and manufacturing processes are expected to conform to the
environmental regulations of the country of origin.

Hodder & Stoughton Ltd
338 Euston Road
London NW1 3BH

www.hodder.co.uk

To all the fans of the show —
thank you for watching.

And to Gareth Carrivick — forever missed.

Contents

How It All Started   2

Series One, Episode One: DATE   8

Series Two, Episode One: THE NEW ME   56

Series Two, Episode Four: A NEW LOW   112

Series Two, Episode Five: JUST ACT NORMAL   164

Series Three, Episode Three: THE DINNER PARTY   212

Series Three, Episode Five: THREE LITTLE WORDS   256

You Have Been Reading . . .   311

Acknowledgements   312

Cast List / Credits   313

How It All Started

Well hello to you dear book purchaser and thank you for your interest in perusing my book o' scripts. I have chosen six of my favourite *Miranda* sitcom scripts from the three series, which include some notes made in rehearsal never seen outside of the sitcom production family. The Series One and Two scripts show how earlier drafts evolved, with some last minute changes – bits that made it, bits that didn't. The two Series Three scripts are exactly what was seen on screen.

It has been a strange process for me, collating these scripts, for a couple of reasons. Firstly, for Series One and Two it has been 5 years and 4 years respectively since I have looked at them. I know they have been repeated on BBC 1 since their first outing on BBC 2 in 2009 and 2010, but I don't tend to look out for myself in the TV schedules and think, 'Oooh, how smashing, I will just sit down with a lovely cuppa and watch me'. That would not lend itself to anything near relaxing. I am a huge fan of television, I have consumed a lot of it over the years, it is probably my favourite art form, particularly the studio audience sitcom, so I don't want to ruin the joy of an evening of it, by the inevitable self-assassination that occurs when you are staring gloomily at your own visage. So, suddenly after half a decade, I am starkly confronted with what I wrote. And forgive me for being frightfully unBritish – hang up your Cath Kidston aprons by the aga and take a pew if you are from the home counties – but I feel a little emotional. A tiny bit moist eyed. The scripts look short, precise, concise and kind of simple in their end form. How I wanted them. But you see, they don't pop out like this. Oh heavens no. There was much angst I put myself through getting them to this stage. Oh deary me, a lot of angst. I was angsty. A giant ball of angst. Angst now seems a very odd word. Angst. Marvellous word – something very angsty about the word angst.

I have made no great secret of the fact that I don't enjoy the writing process. And as I look at the end product I well up as I am immediately transported back to an office at BBC Television Centre and my kitchen table at home and emotionally recall the stress, loneliness, boredom and pressure. The delightful key ingredients that make up my writing process. (Well, probably most writers'.) I put a huge amount of pressure on myself with this sitcom. I didn't want to let TV audiences down, myself down, the BBC down, and blow the opportunity. It had been a long time coming.

Fifteen years before the sitcom first aired in 2009, I had done the first of my ten Edinburgh Festivals to get in to comedy and acting, and I had only given up office work four years before. In retrospect this was a good thing – it gave me time to hone the character that eventually became Miranda in the sitcom. A producer at the BBC, Jo Sargent, saw one of my Edinburgh shows and asked me to come up with a comedy format – it took me a couple of years on and off to work out what project was best for me and, when I had decided on a sitcom, to then work out what was the right setting and characters to serve this on-screen persona. Next I wrote a pilot script which was then commissioned officially by the BBC, initially called *Miranda Hart's Joke Shop* (thank goodness my producer pushed me to rename it). The next development stage is a read through. A read through in a corporate meeting room not in any way conducive to comedy, to which the channel controller, comedy commissioner, and/or other executives are invited to watch and pass judgment on whether a pilot and or series should be commissioned. I had acted in a couple of other people's read throughs before – sat in a row, reading from the scripts, trying to make a busy controller of a TV channel chortle – and it was at best as cringey as farting in a lift with the man you had an embarrassing date with the night before, smiling at him and then realising an hour later you had a large bit of something green in your teeth. I knew I had to do something a little bit different. I asked the producer if we could do the read through at the end of the day, called the actors in as early as possible and spent the whole day rehearsing it with them. Putting it on its feet, acting it out as much as possible, to give it something resembling a chance. Essentially, making it as much of a play as we could do in a day, and indeed in a meeting room. We were then lucky that a lot of people were around that afternoon so instead of the usual two mates and six executives, we had 30 people in the room, so there was less likelihood of shyness if somebody actually did want to laugh. And luckily they did. And a pilot was commissioned. I believe the read through was Autumn 2007 and we filmed the pilot in February 2008. As a side note, I am eternally grateful to the actors – my friends – who did the read through, including Emma Kennedy, Katherine Parkinson, Katherine Jakeways, Alex Lowe and my sister.

Two months later – April 2008 – I was told that BBC 2 wanted a full series. I remember being on the set of another show for ITV called *Monday Monday* when I heard. Tom Ellis happened to be in the show too so I could share my bewilderment and excitement with him. I celebrated for about an hour and then sunk in to an immediate decline. I shall explain forthwith. Before finding out about the TV commission, a radio producer who had been at the read through asked if I wanted to do the show on Radio 2. I was a little hesitant as I had written a visual show, it was always very much a TV commission, and I wondered, if it didn't get picked up by TV, whether my heart would be in it as a radio project. However, it was too good an opportunity to say no to. So between filming the pilot and finding out about the full commission I had started writing the Radio 2 series. And, surprise surprise, I was not enjoying it. For starters I had never written a sitcom before. I had only written one episode. I was on a gigantic learning curve. There were so many technicalities to it. Every story was like a jigsaw puzzle, one thing went wrong or didn't connect and it would fall apart like a house of cards. It wasn't just a case of linking a series of funny happenings, it was objectives and through-lines and making it real as well as laugh-out-loud funny. Sitcoms are a deeply complex beast.

It was hard bloody work to write four episodes for radio (which I am pleased to say we just managed to make work as a radio series, although the 'oops, I have just fallen over' and loud thud sound effects will always make me cringe). Now I had to write six for TV. It was the dream. Yes, absolutely it was. But at the time I was Miss Struggles-To-See-The-Positive-In-Anything at your service, so I went with 'well, it's never going to get written' 'it's going to be rubbish' 'I will get this opportunity and blow it' 'what on earth will all my friends in comedy say' 'oh my poor family'. Then I slapped myself in the face and had 25 glasses of cava and knew I would truly regret it if I didn't give it my best shot. What's the point in kowtowing to a fear of failure? Surely one of the most debilitating of all fears. It's just going to be one series, I mulled, it hopefully won't be too embarrassing, a few members of the WI might like it. Just go for it and hopefully you will still get acting work after a failed self-penned series. Looking on the bright side as ever.

After my one hour of celebration (which involved a mini-roll and a cup of on-set lukewarm tea in a polystyrene cup), and finishing *Monday Monday*, I went to work. I locked myself away, and worked out the rules to sitcom. I was going to say there is no book for this, but there are some books for this, but none that I found particularly helpful. I watched some sitcoms of days gone by – I was concerned about being influenced by any peers. And eventually I got a sense of how the mechanics of a sitcom worked generally. But then I had to work out how I would subvert them, put my own twist on it, how I would make my own particular rules for my own particular show. More pressure. The number-one rule being no self indulgence: picture an audience member holding the remote control hovering over the programme change button and don't let them switch over. Keep their interest, keep them laughing. Further pressure.

So, yes, it is a little emotional seeing these scripts now. Rarely have they been in this clean, polished state. Not really until the day of recording. Even then we might be tweaking. All I remember about scripts are the painful weeks of generating ideas, then months of story-lining, all the graphs and jigsaws of that, then the overlong first drafts (sometimes I would write up to double before cutting down), the polishing of a joke and fearing it was going to die in front of the studio audience, the painful phrasing and rephrasing of every sentence, the poring over every word. All the angst. And the teary-ness comes, I suppose, from the fact that it came together. The scripts now actually exist like this. And here's the proof. And this is the first time I have ever seen them finished. Big sigh.

The second reason it is strange looking at my words now, is because following on from the above, I think for the first time I can feel pride. I know, watch out: deeply unBritish self-congratulation alert. If you are reading this in the home counties this time steady yourself with a scone, an Earl Grey, and stroke the Horse and Hound – magazine and/or actual. But a few years on, I am thinking: be brave, Hart, pat yourself on the back. I told a tiny porky pie at the beginning of this introduction when I said I had never watched the show back when it had been repeated. There was one occasion recently when I was home alone, picked up the remote and started to see what was on. And the first thing I tuned in to was BBC 1 and well, me. I did a panic reflex and changed the channel. And then I risked flicking back. And watched all I could bear of it. (About two and a half minutes.) It was possible to watch as I felt so removed from the person on the screen. It was Series One so I had moved on. The character had moved on. There was enough distance to not be so self-critical. I let go of all the nasty things I had read or heard. I let go of all the embarrassment I felt at my work being recognised and successful. All the worry of Tall Poppy Syndrome. All the anger of people judging and misjudging, quoting and misquoting, convinced it was canned laughter, as-suming it was mainly all improvised on the day (even TV journalists) – OK maybe there is a little anger left about that. (All this and more is for another time!) I let go of all the angst and allowed myself a quiet 'Well done, you did it'. I put the work in and I feel very very lucky that audiences connected with the show, that I got the chance to do three series and, naff as it may sound, to make people laugh. Because that was the main reason I did it.

I still think I don't fully connect to the success of writing three series. As I look at these scripts I can't quite believe they came from my silly mind and that people found them funny and that was down to stupid old me. At this point I have to acknowledge and thank the writers who were brave enough to continue helping me with the series: James Cary, Richard Hurst, Georgia Pritchett, Paul Powell and Paul Kerensa. Forever indebted. I never really own the success of the show, but with this book I am doing as much as I can to. And indeed to encourage other British women to pat themselves on their respective backs too. It's allowed. I say so! For goodness' sake, men might congratulate themselves for peeing straight, or throwing a peanut in the air and catching it in their mouths, yet female heads of corporations might apologise five times a day for having their job. I have gone off piste to a feminist black run. Again, for another time.

Back to this here book in which follow six scripts with introductions by moi, and some other tit-bits, and silliness. Because no book of this ilk should be without tit-bits and silliness. If nothing else it's fun to say tit-bits. Repeat after me: tit-bits. You're welcome. I hope you enjoy seeing the scripts in their pure written form on the page before they translated to what you have seen on screen. And if you're a lovely young person still at school please let me know if your drama teacher ever lets you do an episode for the school play. Nothing would make me happier. Though I bagsy play Miranda.

Date

It made sense to start this book with Series One, Episode One. This started as the pilot episode. The story remained pretty much the same but the characters had developed and changed a little mainly because I had got to know Tom Ellis, Patricia Hodge and last but by no means least tiny Miss Sarah Hadland from the radio series. The latter who had the most influence on her part: tiny Miss Stevie Sutton. Stevie in the pilot was a very serious, suited character whose mission in life was to win *The Apprentice*. She had no sense of humour and was constantly disappointed in Miranda. But I realised watching the pilot back that Miranda needed an ally. (By the way sorry if it's weird for you, but I am used to me calling myself Miranda in this context! I have been known in meetings to say 'no Miranda wouldn't do that' and only realise later that people may think I have gone deeply grand slash insane.) With Penny constantly disappointed and ashamed by her daughter, Tilly showing up her lack of social skills, and Gary not understanding her, there was going to be too much negativity around our central character. So she needed a warm friendship. Studio sitcoms need warmth and heart. And luckily Sarah and I became friends within about two and a half seconds, despite having only met at the audition, much to the alarm of most people around us. There were instant hysterics around the stupidest things, an obsession with animals, impressions, songs (including Sarah bursting in to "what have you done today to make you feel proud") and dancing. An instant childlike kinship. I couldn't have got luckier. The same with all my cast.

I remember being very worried about Patricia Hodge, who I had barely got to know doing the Radio 2 series. We were all still a little intimidated by working with such a sophisticated, elegant, acclaimed star of stage and screen and I was very grateful to her for taking the plunge in to my comedy (not a euphemism). But on the first day of shooting, we were doing some exterior shots and it was the scene where Penny had to faint and collapse on to a pavement on seeing Miranda wearing a wedding dress. So her first experience of the show was lying on a dirty pavement in Hounslow with a camera up her nose. I was dying inside. Now I know Patricia is game for pretty much anything (well not anything, steady on) but I was very concerned she might quit at that point.

Script-wise, it was a difficult episode to write because there was the pressure to grab the audience, to set up all the central characters and establish the situation whilst making sure that was done in a story as if the audience had just jumped in to the world, rather than hideous over-exposition and introductions. Tone-wise, I remember being concerned about Miranda being too self-effacing. I wanted her to be recogniseable to men and women alike as a 30-something who hasn't quite got the confidence to deal with her slightly unusual physical presence. That is a big part of her life and some comedy should come from it. From the fact that she wasn't ready to be 'sexy' which I believe is a very real thing for a lot of women (and indeed men) up to varying points in their life. But it had to be funny. The rule was: no pity. So if the audience ever went 'aaaah' instead of laughing then we would rewrite or perform it in a different way. I think it only ever happened once. And once Stevie got a 'boo' for being rude to Miranda. We took that out and I had to work on the tone of Miranda and Stevie lovingly teasing rather than ever being offensive to each other. It was a celebration of women and all their marvelous different forms, not an attack.

Talking of not feeling sexy and appearances, my favourite scene in this episode to film – and a deeply cathartic life moment – was the cut away of Miranda doing her own version of a Trinny and Susannah-style clothes programme. Here is Episode One, Series One. Enjoy.

INT. MIRANDA'S SITTING ROOM

MIRANDA: (TO CAMERA) Hello to you and thanks for joining. This is exciting isn't it? Eh? Now let me get you up to speed. Previously in my life, my mother tried to marry me off.

EXT. OXFORD STREET (FLASHBACK)

We see a man holding a golf sale sign.

Then we see Penny, Miranda's mother, also holding a sign.

Hers reads 'bridal sale'.

PENNY: (THROUGH MEGAPHONE) Someone please marry my daughter… I'm not asking for money… I'm literally giving her away.

We follow the arrow of Penny's sign and discover an embarrassed Miranda forced to stand next to it.

INT. MIRANDA'S SITTING ROOM

Back to present.

MIRANDA: (TO CAMERA) She was upset because I'd just told her how I'd blown my inheritance. I bought a joke shop. Oops. No, I love it. Although I'm worried that hiring my oldest friend to manage it was a mistake.

Cut to:

Production Note
make sure shop set is
pretty & not corporate

INT. MIRANDA'S SHOP (FLASHBACK)

We see Stevie at a flip chart.

STEVIE: And that is how we will take this franchise global.

She is shouting business-isms. 'We need a bigger profit margin', 'come on people' type stuff.

We reveal she's just talking to Miranda in the shop who is sitting on a joke chair.

MIRANDA: It's a bit much isn't it (TO A STUFFED KANGAROO). I mean we're just a little shop that sells…

STEVIE: Shush and submit… (SOUNDING A LOUD KLAXON)

Miranda falls off chair.

Cut to:

INT. MIRANDA'S SITTING ROOM

Back to present.

MIRANDA: (TO CAMERA) And today I'm overexcited because apparently Gary Preston is back from his travels. He's lovely. But I always make a cock up if I see him. Well there's never any cock up involved, if you see what I mean… how naughty. Oh, but the last time I saw him… (CRINGES)

Cut to:

INT. PARTY (FLASHBACK - 3 YEARS AGO)

GARY: Come on, we've got to dance to this one.

MIRANDA: Ooh OK.

There are a group of people dancing.

Miranda is wearing an elasticated-waist skirt or trousers.
She is sitting on a chair.

Gary comes and asks her to dance. She stands up and starts dancing.
Her skirt/trousers fall down revealing some sizeable pants.

Miranda doesn't realise for a bit and keeps dancing. Then realises.

Cut to:

INT. MIRANDA'S SITTING ROOM

Back to present.

MIRANDA: (TO CAMERA) (STILL CRINGEING) Say nothing. We'll speak no more of and let's crack on with the show...

Title music and scene.

ASK HADDERS IF OK TO USE. THINK HER TURN OF PHRASE.

Cut to:

INT. MIRANDA'S JOKE SHOP

A boutique joke/party/gift shop. It's colourful and welcoming. Big, with wooden floors. A unique boutique with wooden shelves and chests.

It sells balloons, banners, costumes and jokes; but also 'smarter' things for birthday gifts.

There is a laptop on the till area and a small kitchen area in a back room.

Stevie is stock-taking. A few boxes of stock have arrived – including a box of chocolate willies.

Miranda comes downstairs.

MIRANDA: Morning Stevie.

STEVIE: Afternoon. It's nearly lunchtime.

MIRANDA: Oh the trains were a nightmare. It was a hellish journey.

STEVIE: You live upstairs.

MIRANDA: There were leaves on the carpet... (OFF STEVIE'S LOOK) That was a good one – what's up with you?

STEVIE: It's delivery day, and you were going to help. (BEAT)

~~I'm feeling hot and anxious. Like a... mouse in a microwave.
Can't even do an analogy.~~ *TOO WEIRD SO EARLY ON. SAVE FOR ANOTHER SCRIPT.*

Right, you can make a start with the chocolate penises.

MIRANDA: (LAUGHING) Sorry. Every time. They're like willies...
but chocolate.

Stevie looks fed up.

Stevie, they're funny, they're like willies with chocolate. (LAUGHS)
Nothing from you. Quite realistic aren't they.

STEVIE: Not really no.

MIRANDA: Aren't they? (LOOKS TO CAMERA)

STEVIE: (BEAT) Can you just, just concentrate.

MIRANDA: But it's nearly lunchtime. I'm meant to be having a reunion
lunch with the girls.

STEVIE: But you hate the girls.

MIRANDA: I know, but as Tilly says, 'When you're dumped in a boarding
school dorm aged nine you all bond for life even if you hate each other'. Or
in my case get embarrassed being out with people with public school
nicknames. In my class, Milly, Tilly, Bella, Bunty, Hooty,
Pussy, Puggle and Podge. No you're right I'm not going.

STEVIE: Good girly. Work not shirk. Or do you want our business to fold?

MIRANDA: My business.

STEVIE: On paper, but I manage the shop, it's my reputation on the line.

MIRANDA: Do the analogy I like.

STEVIE: OK… (ACTING IT OUT) you're the simple, hulking giant, galumphing along with your money sack, but I'm the ingenious little leprechaun… top of the morning…

MIRANDA: (JOINING IN) Top of the morning…

STEVIE: Just me. (BEAT) Top of the morning… (IN NORMAL ACCENT) And I spin our funds into gold. (BEAT) What do you spin?

WAIT UNTIL THEY KNOW CHARACTERS BETTER FOR THIS KIND OF DIALOGUE

MIRANDA: Preferably hamsters. In a wheel. That is fun. Weeee — they whiz round gripping their tiny claws to the wheel of terror. (OFF STEVIE'S LOOK) An assistant in my own shop. It don't go making no sense.

STEVIE: Until we can afford a proper assistant.

TOO SURREAL

Delivery man comes in.

MIRANDA: I'll get it.

She signs for a number of boxes.

DELIVERY MAN: Thank you sir.

He smiles, nods at Miranda and leaves.

MIRANDA: (TO CAMERA) Did he just call me sir? He just called me sir.

Stevie is laughing.

I mean it's fine if they're not really looking, notice the height, call me sir, look up, 'oh sorry Madam'. That happens. But he looked straight at me and still thought Sir was the right option. (BEAT) Right, that's it. As a girl, I'm going to my girly lunch.

STEVIE: Tell you what…

Unzips Miranda's cardigan

Why don't you get these out – honk honk (HER BREASTS)?
Might help…

Penny sweeps in.

17

PENNY: Miranda…?

MIRANDA: Oh morning, Mum. How are you?

PENNY: Are you engaged yet?

MIRANDA: Not since you asked last night, no. And I said, good morning Mum, how are you?

PENNY: Don't get emotional. We're not Spanish. (BEAT) So, news just in, call me Fiona Bruce…

MIRANDA/STEVIE: Fiona Bruce. (THEY HIGH FIVE EACH OTHER)

PENNY: Benjy has at last split up from that ghastly fish woman.

MIRANDA: I've said it before, I'll say it again, I'm not marrying my cousin.

PENNY: It didn't stop Uncle John and Aunt Liz. They're very happy.

MIRANDA: Yes but their son isn't.

PENNY: Far too fussy, this is Surrey, no one minds – such fun!

Penny exits.

STEVIE: (ANNOYED) This isn't our delivery. (TAKES OUT BABY CLOTHES AND TOYS) Right, this very much needs sorting out.

MIRANDA: Right. (BEAT) I'm off. (OFF STEVIE'S LOOK) My lunch is very important. It's what us elegant girls about town do.

STEVIE: Don't you mean 'Elephant' girls? (LAUGHS)
Oh, I've amused myself.

MIRANDA: Well at least I'm not too small that I can't get on all the rides at
Thorpe Park.

STEVIE: (BEAT) Well at least I don't have to go to specialist clothes
shops… Where are those jeans from?

MIRANDA: (QUIETLY) Big'N'Long.

STEVIE: Sorry?

MIRANDA: Big'N'Long. Well, doesn't mean I can't be feminine.

*Miranda picks up her coat and tries to flounce femininely out,
but falls and knocks a mass of boxes over.*

Look at that, yeah, working it.

Quickly gets up and poses.

It's all about the recovery.

Turns, immediately falls over something else.

Jumps up again — has a chocolate willy on a stick this time.

Cut to:

EXT. STREET BY RESTAURANT

Miranda outside the restaurant.

MIRANDA: (TO CAMERA) How could a man think a woman is a man?

I mean I do have a penis – but that's chocolate. (STARTS TO EAT IT) Ooh actually, that would look wrong in public.

She looks around deciding where to put it. A woman walks past with an open bag over her shoulder. Miranda puts it in there and runs off.

Cut to:

INT. RESTAURANT

Miranda is hanging up her coat. Gary comes out of the kitchen.

MIRANDA: No way – Gary Preston. Ooh, OK calm, compose myself. Smile.

Miranda starts smiling and getting into a 'cool' position.

She grins so much that she looks strained when Gary turns round to see her.

GARY: Miranda? Hi, how are you? Are you OK? You look like you're in pain.

MIRANDA: No, no I'm fine, it's just trapped wind… Ah, that's better. (BEAT) So Gary… What are you doing here?

GARY: I work here – I'm the new chef. Started last week. BETTER EXPLAIN SHOP & RESTAURANT LOCATION.

MIRANDA: Oh wow, my shop's next door.

GARY: No way! It's great to see you. It's been ages.

Gary goes in to kiss her cheek but Miranda arranges it so they end up kissing on the lips.

Have you been eating chocolate?

MIRANDA: Well to be precise, it's actually coc… cockolate. So, how was Malaysia?

GARY: Yeah great, great. It's good to get back though.

MIRANDA: Really?

GARY: Well you know, you can have too much fun. Thought I'd come back and settle down a bit. Be sensible… Joined the gym today…

MIRANDA: Oh, the one round the corner…

GARY: Yeah, do you go?

MIRANDA: Loads. (TO CAMERA) Never. (TO GARY) Yeah no I'm really into keeping fit.

GARY: Great, what's your sport?

MIRANDA: Gymnastics. That's it. I'll work with that. I am a gymnast, Gary.

GARY: Wow.

MIRANDA: Wow indeed. Yeah, I mainly do ribbons (DEMONSTRATES), you might have seen me at the last Olympics. Although having said that I wasn't on telly much because you will have noticed that a lot of gymnasts are quite manly, no curves or breasts, well that's one category. Not mine. I'm in the bustier section. Less televised. Only in widescreen. Gymnasts – busty, is the category.

Awkward pause. Miranda clocks camera.

GARY: Right, right, good… Well, I better get back to work… new job and everything. But, er, let's catch up soon… yes. (GOES)

MIRANDA: (TO CAMERA) Well that all went very well. Luckily I enjoy living alone.

Mix to:

INT. MIRANDA'S FLAT (FLASHBACK). NIGHT

How are we going to film this?!

We see Miranda in a boiler suit covered in velcro.

She throws a mass of tennis balls against the wall and tries to get as many as possible on to her body.

Mix to:

INT. RESTAURANT (BACK TO PRESENT)

Miranda starts heading into main bit of restaurant and sees Clive sitting with a coffee, reading a paper.

MIRANDA: Ooh Clive.

CLIVE: Can't talk now, I'm working. (TURNS NEWSPAPER)

He sees a customer trying to get his attention.

We hear the girls laughing.

MIRANDA: Oh, wish me luck, girl's lunch…

We arrive at the table where we see Tilly and Fanny. Tilly is on her phone.

TILLY: Have to go, here she is, hola! Utmost cooliosity!

MIRANDA: Tilly!

TILLY: It's been forever.

Fanny and Tilly scream.

Miranda gets a fright.

Kissingtons. *(She air kisses)* and... *(pointing to Fanny)*

MIRANDA: Fanny...

FANNY: Queen Kong!

MIRANDA: I prefer Miranda.

TILLY: Oh no, it has to be Queen Kong – you look exactly the same, you're Empress of Kong. (BEAT) Queen Kongalzeeza Rice.

Fanny and Tilly laugh and do a scream.

(She gets a text on her BlackBerry. She picks it up and starts texting.) Oh hang on, bear with, bear with, bear with... *(finishes the text)* back... when they first said that work was moving here I actually considered suicide. Major Suburb-areene. But this *(pointing at the three of them)*, this, is going to be stupendulent.

No time. Save 'stupendent' for Tilly. Great from Sal!

Miranda clocks camera.

MIRANDA: So, what's new?

TILLY: Well...

She excitedly shows her engagement ring.

Fanny does the same.

Miranda lifts up her left hand. There is no ring.

The girls look shocked.

FANNY: Hideola.

TILLY: Poor Kongers.

MIRANDA: No. I'm fine, really pleased for you. Marriage and the baby thing is not for me. Only what my mother wants.

FANNY: Seriously now, is your mum coping OK?

MIRANDA: Oh, she's fine.

Mix to:

INT. PENNY'S DINING ROOM OR SITTING ROOM (FLASHBACK)

Penny is howling.

She sees a photo of Miranda.

She puts it away and replaces it with a new photo.

It's a picture of a black sheep.

Mix back to:

INT. RESTAURANT (BACK TO PRESENT)

FANNY: So Queen Kong, we're arranging a shopping bonanza to...

MIRANDA: Um? Oh, girls' shopping trip – yay!

TILLY: Oh will you come with? Marvellisimus.

They start talking excitedly – a noise of girly incoherence with the odd word coming through like 'taxi-Cola', 'Rigby Peller', 'super-tastic', 'max it up', 'chiffon'.

Miranda clocks camera and does an impression of them.

Suddenly the cacophony stops and Miranda quickly stops her impression with a fake yawn.

TILLY: So I suggest we just meet there tomorrow afternoon, at, shall we say four? (BEAT) Brillo pads.

MIRANDA: Sorry, where are we going, Tilly? I just didn't quite catch it.

FANNY: Wedding dress shopping.

MIRANDA: (TO CAMERA) Kill me.

TOO MANY 'TO CAMERAS' ALREADY?

GARY: Right ladies, what can I get for you – Madam?

MIRANDA: Madam, brilliant. Thanks Gary.

Cut to:

INT. MIRANDA'S SHOP

Boxes of stock everywhere. It's a mess.

Stevie is frazzled, on hold on the phone, trying to tidy etc.

Miranda enters.

MIRANDA: Stevie, Stevie, Stevie, Stevie, Stevie, Stevie etc… I won't stop, Stevie, Stevie, Stevie…

Stevie turns to look at her.

STEVIE: A little bit busy?!

MIRANDA: I just saw Gary. He's working next door.

STEVIE: No way, and?

MIRANDA: I told him I was an Olympic gymnast.

STEVIE: Why?

MIRANDA: You know when you get nervous socially you

end up lying to impress.

STEVIE: No.

MIRANDA: Exactly, we all do it. So what is going on in here?

Stevie looks anxious.

STEVIE: They still haven't taken the baby stuff back, I've been on hold for over an hour, I mean listen to the hold music. (SHE PLAYS IT) It's continuous, I'm going insane… and we've had a double delivery of chocolate peni…

Ghastly plinkety plonk irritating music

Miranda laughs.

Stevie does the klaxon.

MIRANDA: You've never known how to have fun.

STEVIE: I have fun. I host barbecues. (BEAT) They are renowned through-out the shire.

No time in this script. Do another time will need 12 difft. photos of Sarah

MIRANDA: The shire?

STEVIE: (BEAT) Yes the shire. Some of us focus on work. Ever won one of these?

We see an employee of the month board — every month a different photo of Stevie.

STEVIE: Yeah well some of us like to focus on work! Now get round here and help me tidy tidy please!

Stevie starts tidying the till area. Miranda helps. They come across an item that springs out of a box.

They can't get the box closed before it springs out.

STEVIE: You can't get these in…

MIRANDA: Before you put the lid on…

It springs out of the box. They get a fright.

STEVIE: It's quite a nice shock isn't it?

Another one goes off. They scream.

Gary comes in.

GARY: Hello.

Miranda and Stevie scream.

GARY: Sorry, didn't mean to scare you.

Stevie sits on the stool/chair behind the till.

> *All characters should feel physical in the comedy in the show, not just Miranda. This stool push could maybe be a regular thing?*

MIRANDA: No it's fine. Gary, you remember Stevie. Stevie – Gary.

STEVIE: Hello, sorry, we thought you'd come out of Miranda's box.

Miranda pushes her off her stool. She disappears behind till.

GARY: Wow, you seem busy. Things are obviously going well.

MIRANDA: Yep yep yep. Put simply, I'm deeply successful. Yeah, so look around, I'm a cock magnet – shoot me.

GARY: Ummm, look I just popped in to ask, actually, you're not with anybody or married or anything at the moment are you?

MIRANDA: Yep, yep of course, yeah.

GARY: Oh. Really? Kids?

MIRANDA: Yep. We've got two. Um there's Orlando and Bloom. You?

GARY: No, no, still single.

MIRANDA: Me too.

GARY: You just said you were married?

MIRANDA: Divorced now.

GARY: And the kids?

MIRANDA: Dead.

GARY: Really, what happened?

This comes from stand up. Flashback to pub theatres. Eeek, this is harder ..... MH.

MIRANDA: They froze. They froze to death, Gary. It's a funny story actually. Well not funny, ha, ha, but funny in that it's almost unbelievable. We were on holiday in the Himalayas, base camp of Everest and it was really cold and they were just running around in shorts and T-shirt and I kept saying put a coat on, you'll catch your death. And they did...

GARY: (BEAT) None of that is true is it?

MIRANDA: No. You know when you get nervous socially and you end up lying to impress?

GARY: No.

MIRANDA: Exactly we all do it.

Gary laughs.

GARY: Right well look, look, well I wanted to ask, do you want to…?

MIRANDA: Yes.

GARY: I haven't said anything…

MIRANDA: I'll do whatever…

GARY: Do you fancy grabbing a bite later? I'm not working and be good to catch up. We could just go to the restaurant, you know, it's free food, don't worry it's not a date, just a thing, if you like.

MIRANDA: I do like. I do like very much. (TO CAMERA) Why am I doing an Indian accent?

GARY: Cool. right well I'll pop in when I've finished my shift.

MIRANDA: Ciao.

STEVIE: Froze to death?! Orlando and Bloom?!

Cut to:

too "stand-uppy"?

INT. MIRANDA'S SITTING ROOM

MIRANDA: (TO CAMERA) I've got a date. I've got a date! I've got a date! Over excited. That's boarding school education for you. Starved of male company for years, still now when a bloke says 'hi' you think 'nice spring wedding'. (SHE GRABS A BISCUIT) Calm. I'm not even looking for a relationship but Gary is particularly delicious. As is this (THE BISCUIT). Wish it was legal to marry food.

Cut to:

PENNY'S SITTING ROOM

Miranda is hugging a giant/life size pork pie with bow tie.

We see Penny in wedding outfit, screaming with excitement like the girls do.

Cut to:

No time. Too rushed. Need to make sure T & S below stays in edit.

Ooh what to do, OK. What would the girls do? Shopping, of course, something to wear, yes... I will Trinny and Susannah myself. I couldn't do it with them because I'd have to punch them in the face. Hate those kind of programmes. Welcome to I'm OK, you're O-bese. I know what I'd do if I had one of those shows…

Cut to:

EXT. STREET. DAYLIGHT

Miranda with a camera and operator with boom. She goes up to a woman wearing a horrid top and tracksuit bums.

MIRANDA: Ah, excuse me – hello.

WOMAN 2: (LOW MONOSYLABBIC VOICE) Hello.

MIRANDA: Right let's look at you. Well I wouldn't buy that top, but you look comfortable. Are you?

WOMAN 2: Yeah.

MIRANDA: Do you like it?

WOMAN 2: Yeah.

MIRANDA: Do you care others may not like it?

WOMAN 2: No.

MIRANDA: Brilliant, wear that then. Bye. *can't wait to film this!*

INT. MIRANDA'S SHOP

Stevie is on the phone by the till. More boxes have arrived. She is helping a male customer. Miranda comes downstairs. She grabs her jacket and starts to head out.

STEVIE: Errr, where are you going?

MIRANDA: To get something to wear. How often do I have a date? Never, it's my first one!

Customer looks shocked.

MIRANDA: First one of the many others I've also had.

STEVIE: I thought he said it wasn't a date.

MIRANDA: Well he said it was a 'thing'. That's code for date isn't it. I mean (TO CUSTOMER) if you wanted to ask me out, but were intimidated by the natural beauty, (BEAT) you'd say 'thing' not 'date' wouldn't you?

The customer is about to speak.

Miranda puts her hand over his mouth, and nods his face up and down speaking for him:

'Yes I would.'

STEVIE: Just don't scare him off. And you can help me before you go shopping. We've had another delivery of baby stock and the hen night stock's still not here. And I'm not enjoying telling the delivery company we're still missing fluffy handcuffs and love eggs. It's degrading! So no shoppy-shoppy til you tidy-tidy.

MIRANDA: I'm fairly sure that's racist.

The customer leaves. Miranda creeps out, hiding behind him.

STEVIE: Uhh, I can see you...

MIRANDA: (TO CUSTOMER) That was your fault. Get out. (PUSHES HIM OUT)

If people don't get this it's still a good M & Stevie relationship thing. Risk it!

STEVIE: Don't you want to achieve? I always think big, and then I think Small. Heather Small. (BEAT) I ask myself (SINGING) 'what have you done today to make you feel proud'(BEAT). What are you going to say?

MIRANDA: Fine, I'd say Heather, Heather Small, you were excellent on *Strictly Come Dancing* (BOTH: Yeah she was wasn't she), and today I helped my lovely little friend by putting the boxes away.

Miranda goes over to the boxes.

STEVIE: Thank you. And not in the (POINTING) kitchen slash work station slash break area slash my personal space.

MIRANDA: (TO STEVIE) Slash. (BEAT) Good word, sorry.

Stevie picks up the phone and turns around to stock check some items behind the till, singing and moving mockingly to the music in her ear.

MIRANDA: Stevie, I wouldn't...

STEVIE: Good, because I wouldn't put them in your flat, slash...

MIRANDA: (TO CAMERA) Slash

STEVIE: ...personal space.

MIRANDA: No, exactly so I wouldn't do that to you...

Stevie still singing, back to Miranda.

Miranda throws the boxes into the kitchen.

Penny enters.

PENNY: Forgot to say earlier. I'm going to the baby shop to get a present for cousin Georgina's christening tomorrow. Very anti-social to have it on a, what I call, weekday.

MIRANDA: It is a weekday. Not just what you call a weekday. It is a weekday. I mean, that is such an annoying, what I call, phrase.

PENNY: (BEAT) Shall I get you something to give them?

MIRANDA: I didn't know there was a christening.

PENNY: I don't know what I'm going to get them. Such an ugly baby. Your father suggested a balaclava! Such fun! Right, well I must dash, meeting someone for a spot of, what I call, tea.

MIRANDA: It is tea.

Stevie still on the phone, by till, with her back to main bit of shop.

Miranda realises she can leave without Stevie noticing.

MIRANDA: Stevie, I've tidy-tidied!

Runs out.

EXT. BUSY HIGH STREET

Miranda walking along.

MIRANDA: (TO CAMERA) Right, clothes shops. I've been to Big 'N' Long – nothing. Just because people are taller or bigger than average, why do we have to shop in patronisingly named places. What's next, Lanky 'N' Sweaty, Swallowers and Amazonians, Huge 'N' Gross…

She sees and approaches a shop called 'Trans-formers'. The sign in the window reads 'bespoke ladies tailoring. Shoe sizes up to 14. Dress sizes up to 48 chest.'

MIRANDA: Big sizes for once, perfect.

Miranda is not aware that the shop is for men to women transformations.

A man with stubble, but in a dress, with a handbag walks out. Miranda is still looking in the window so doesn't notice him.

She goes into the shop thinking it's for women. The shop has dark windows and is obviously low key.

INT. TRANS-FORMER SHOP

SHOP ASSISTANT: Hi there. How can we help?

Hope we get Patrick Barlow to play this. Love him.

MIRANDA: Oh, hi, yes. I'm looking for something flattering for me and really feminine. Because, this might sound ridiculous, but I often get called sir – I know, embarrassing – and I'm going out tonight and don't want it to happen then.

SHOP ASSISTANT: I hear you. (WINKS) Let's have a look at you. Well you are naturally very feminine. You're lucky. Shapely. Lady-like curves and as for those. (HER BREASTS) Astonishing. I've seen quite a few in my time but these are something else.

MIRANDA: Oh, thanks.

SHOP ASSISTANT: Good hair. Where did you get it?

MIRANDA: My father's side.

SHOP ASSISTANT: Oh, I haven't heard of them.

Miranda looks a bit confused.

SHOP ASSISTANT: Right. Well, it's not going to take much... Heads will turn, and not in a pointing-and-staring way.

MIRANDA: I always knew I could pull it off but didn't know what clothes would suit me best.

SHOP ASSISTANT: Well there is no point in wearing jeans and a T-shirt is there, you might as well be a man.

Now, let's sort you out for tonight, young lady.

He emphasises 'lady' laughingly

Miranda looks excited to camera.

MIRANDA: (IN AMERICAN ACCENT) Ooh, lady!

He laughs and touches her arm and she does it back.

Cut to:

INT. MIRANDA'S SHOP

Stevie is still on hold at the till. The shop is still a mess. A customer, Paul (gay man), is browsing.

Miranda peers inside the door.

MIRANDA: Stevie, I've got an outfit. Are you ready?

Miranda enters.

The outfit and make-up are so over the top — a Danny la Rue number. She looks like a transvestite.

STEVIE: (LOOKING DOWN) Just give me a second!

MIRANDA: So, how do I look! (SEEING PAUL) Sorry. Didn't realise anyone was here.

PAUL: No problem. Wow. Can I just say. You look gorgeous.

MIRANDA: Ahhh, thank you.

PAUL: It's amazing. So feminine.

MIRANDA: Stop it!

PAUL: No, seriously. I mean you could pass.

MIRANDA: Really, I could pass could I?! Brilliant.
(TO CAMERA) I passed.

Stevie looks up.

STEVIE: Miranda, why are you dressed as a transvestite?

PAUL: (BEAT) I am so sorry... I thought...

MIRANDA: Just get out please. (HE GOES)

STEVIE: (BEAT) Don't worry. (TRYING NOT TO LAUGH) Didn't he just say you looked gorgeous and feminine?

MIRANDA: As a *man*, Stevie. For a *man* he thought I was gorgeous and feminine. For a man. As a man. A man. As a man. Are you laughing?

STEVIE: (LAUGHS) No. (TRYING TO SUPRESS) There is nothing funny here.

MIRANDA: There isn't, because I wear normal everyday clothes and I get called sir. I actually make an effort and…

As she says the following Gary comes in.

MIRANDA: I am a transvestite.

GARY: Hi.

MIRANDA: (TURNS TO FACE GARY) Hi.

GARY: Oh – did we say it was fancy dress tonight…?

STEVIE: No, this isn't fancy…

MIRANDA: Yes it is. Was just trying on our new range of…(LOOKS TO STEVIE FOR HELP)

STEVIE: Transvestite costumes…

MIRANDA: (TAKES STEVIE ASIDE AND WHISPERS) How does that help?

STEVIE: I don't know, I'm panicking.

MIRANDA: *You're* panicking. (EMPHATICALLY WITHOUT SAYING ANYTHING POINTS OUT HER DRESS)

STEVIE: (BEAT) It'll all be fine. Just be yourself.

MIRANDA: What an appalling piece of advice. (GOES BACK TO GARY)

GARY: (BEAT) Shall I just come back…?

MIRANDA: No, two seconds… just get changed.

Hushed & rushed between them

Add in:-

STEVIE: Oh Miranda, I can't believe you filled my personal space!

41

MIRANDA: This is not the time. (TO GARY) That is not what it sounds.*

MIRANDA: I'll be two seconds, I'll just…

She tires to flounce femininely upstairs, but gets caught up and falls over as she does.

*
Think rhythm in
performance.

Cut to:

See in the edit
if we need this.
Depends how well
audience reacts
to the clowning.
Be good MH!

INT. RESTAURANT

Gary and Miranda at the end of their meal.

MIRANDA: …and how did you end up being a chef…

GARY: I just picked it up when I was travelling really, worked in lots of restaurants. Yeah, I've really got into it. I feel like I've finally found what I want to do…

MIRANDA: That's great. So your parents must be pleased you're back… how's your mum?

GARY: Still frantically trying to find me a wife.

MIRANDA: My mother's the same.

GARY: What, trying to find you a wife…

MIRANDA: (LAUGHING) Finding me a wife… but just to be clear, she wants to find me a husband… because I am a woman.

Gary thinks she's joking, Miranda isn't so he stops laughing.

INT. MIRANDA'S SHOP. NIGHT.

They walk across the shop floor.

GARY: Exactly. And it's not just marriage, it's the desperation to have kids...

MIRANDA: I know. I just don't have that desperate urge to breed... I'm up here (POINTING UPSTAIRS)... if we did have a desperate urge to breed... we could... (TO CAMERA) Why? He's gone up!

They go upstairs.

Running up as fast as possible might be funny.

INT. OUTSIDE MIRANDA'S FLAT

Miranda gets her keys out.

GARY: ...the number of women who turn thirty and they're suddenly obsessed with babies.

MIRANDA: I know, I mean it's so boring. I'd say I have a fairly normal, healthy interest in children...

Opens her door and switches on the light.

The room is full of baby stuff.

There are prams, cots, dummies, clothes, mobiles etc.

Everywhere.

They stare at it. Long pause.

GARY: Well, it's getting late.

MIRANDA: Bye... (HE GOES)

43

Cut to:

INT. MIRANDA'S SHOP

Stevie is working. The shop is all tidy now. The radio is on.

Miranda comes down the stairs and blasts the klaxon at Stevie.

MIRANDA: You ruined my chances last night. Turns out a flat full of baby stock isn't an aphrodisiac.

STEVIE: Gary was in your flat? What, was he lost? (BEAT)

Miranda smiles sarcastically at Stevie, who smiles back.

Cut to Miranda then back to Stevie.

Sorry I didn't think he'd come back. And you shouldn't have put it all in (POINTING TO KITCHEN) my personal space.

MIRANDA: Sorry. Well everything seems tidy-tidy in here now.

STEVIE: They finally picked up the extra penises. And I've had a call from the baby shop. All that stuff upstairs is theirs and they've got our hen night stock.

She hears a good boppy song on the radio.

STEVIE: Oh, this is a good tune.

Starts dancing with a dance face.

MIRANDA: You're doing your dance face.

STEVIE: Everyone has a dance face.

Let's rehearse & learn a routine to try in front of audience but make sure we can edit out for time.

MIRANDA: I deliberately don't because they're so embarrassing.

Dances with a dance face.

PENNY: (PANICKED) Miranda, you are in a street with some very dodgy businesses – that baby shop, I've just come from the christening. Marjorie gave a silver incrusted rattle, Victoria an engraved mug, I presented what I thought was a lovely toy rabbit – turns out it was a battery operated (MOUTHS) sex toy. Worst thing was, the baby loved it! Couldn't prize it off him! It was absolutely, what I call, mortifying. (BEAT)

INT. RESTAURANT

Miranda is leaning at the bar trying to act cool.

CLIVE: What are you doing?

MIRANDA: Being nonchalant for Gary.

CLIVE: Good luck.

GARY: Miranda?

MIRANDA: Oh hello Gary, fancy seeing you here.

GARY: I work here.

MIRANDA: Isn't that weird, of all the restaurants I could have popped in to…

GARY: But I work here and you know that…

MIRANDA: (LOUDLY OVER HIM) It's all just very weird.

GARY: I was coming to see you later. I was an idiot last night, running away before you could explain…

MIRANDA: …it was a stock mix-up you see, and…

GARY: You don't need to say. But you do need to let me take you out for a drink later.

MIRANDA: OK.

GARY: Great, great. Was there anything else, you don't want to order some food?

MIRANDA: Do you do wedding cakes? Oh no, no, um that was just a joke.

That's the worst kind of joke I could have made. Don't worry, you know I'm not into all that. Laters...

She bumps and trips over the coatstand.

Cut to:

could maybe try carrying out coat stand in rehearsals!!

INT. WEDDING DRESS SHOP

Tilly and Fanny are in their wedding dresses. Miranda enters.

MIRANDA: Sorry I'm late. Wow, you all look great.

They all laugh excitedly. Fanny is holding a glass of champagne.

TILLY: We're amongst friends, so I can say this…

Fanny still laughing.

Ssh Fanny… I can be honest – I don't think I've ever felt more beautiful. (BEAT) Kong creature, you've got to try one, it's the most amazing experi-ence, it's better than anything horse!

MIRANDA: Be a bit weird with no engagement ring.

Shop assistant comes in.

SHOP ASSISTANT: Hello sir.

MIRANDA: Right I will. I would like to try one on please.

SHOP ASSISTANT: Really? (LOOKS AT MIRANDA PROPERLY) Oh sorry… I think I might have something… size?

MIRANDA: Ten.

Everyone stares.

Ten…ty. I mean twenty.

SHOP ASSISTANT: Yes, I think we've got one in a size… tenty… (SHE GOES)

Time passes. The girls and shop assistant are now waiting outside a dressing room. It opens and Miranda comes out in the biggest meringue dress ever.

MIRANDA: I'm amongst friends so I can be honest; I don't think I've ever felt more beautiful.

TILLY: Really?

MIRANDA: No, I look like I've had a chiffon-based anaphylactic shock.
Be a nightmare if my mother walked past now. She'd faint with joy.

Gary appears at the window.

No!

Gary walks quickly on. Miranda is about to leave the shop to go after him when she sees Penny walk past, who faints with joy.

(TO CAMERA) This is almost getting ridiculous.

Turns to run out of the shop

Gary, wait!

Cut to:

EXT. STREET

Gary sees Miranda coming out of the shop. He starts running. Miranda chases.

MIRANDA: Come back. I am not desperate. What are you so scared of? Gary, come back.

End music comes in.

'You have been watching' comes on screen...

*We see Miranda running along, and 'Miranda Hart' comes up on screen.
She waves to camera.*

*We see Gary running, looking scared at what's behind him, and 'Tom Ellis'
comes up on screen. He acknowledges camera.*

*We see Penny on the pavement, coming round and 'Patricia Hodge'
comes up on screen. She looks to camera.*

*We see the girls peering out of the shop, with their names on the screen.
They wave to camera.*

*We cut to the shop and Stevie is on hold (as if earlier action).
'Sarah Hadland' comes up on screen. She looks at camera.*

We see Miranda chasing Gary.

MIRANDA: Gaaaarrrryyyy…

Series One, Episode One:
Behind the Scenes Tit-Bits.

Tom Ellis was the first person to corpse (get the giggles) when filming in front of the live audience. It was during my speech in the restaurant about being a gymnast and I suddenly did some movement with the imaginary ribbons that I had never done in rehearsals and he went. I was secretly thrilled I had got him!

Patricia Hodge was second and couldn't get out the line about the toy rabbit towards the end of the episode. When she first came in to say that line she split it up so the audience could see what was coming. They started laughing and then Patricia lost it.

Nick Frost came up with the name Queen Kong for me when we were doing a sitcom called *Hyperdrive* together. Thanks Nick.

We had to re-shoot the chocolate willy scene when I am walking down the street because the show ended up being scheduled at 8.30 p.m. when they thought it would be 9p.m. Lovely Janice Hadlow, the then controller of BBC 2 thought the willy we first shot was a little too 'anatomically correct'. That was an awkward meeting.

Could this be the time to model?

Unamused by the notion of swinging

This is much easier and more fun than skiing

Let's move swiftly on...

These are the photos that appear in the title sequence of the show. We made the title sequence very short because the pilot that became Episode One was over running, so we only had time to do a 10 – 11 second intro which meant we flicke...

Giggling at my sisters bowl cut: 'No seriously, it looks fine'

A bit of twenty-something 'tude

Clearly never been happier

Fancy dress as <u>what?</u>

...through the photos
very quickly much to
my relief. We then
stuck with that for the
rest of the series but
here you get to see
the photos in all their
glory. Excuse me whilst
I just hide under my sofa
cushion in a cringe ball.

Miranda

Look everyone it only took me
19 months but I can now walk

'It was <u>this</u> big'

I have never felt
more beautiful

The New Me

. . .

Aaah, the tricky second album… And the first episode of the tricky second album certainly brought with it the aforementioned angst. I think the fabulous writers who helped me storyline, Messers James Cary and Richard Hurst could testify to a little bit of 'going mad' for this series and in particular this episode. But it was to be the test as to whether those audience members who stuck with Series One were going to stick with Series Two. You didn't want to get X number of viewers on week one and then lose half of them on week two. A writer's nightmare.

I had left Series One on a bit of a cliffhanger in terms of Miranda trying to tell Gary she loved him, not having the guts and Gary leaving to go to Hong Kong. (Deliberately wrote that to persuade the BBC we needed another series!) And it's always important to leave a series with a question mark so you don't have the excuse of not writing again. So there was an obvious beginning to Series Two of Miranda in a right old state having lost out on the potential love of her life. And someone having let themselves go felt like a good place to go comedically particularly with this character and the fun that her mother and Tilly would have with her as a total mess. Plus you could make life as bad as possible for your central character before things started looking up. It was fairly easy to then suggest Penny coming to live with her — a fussy mother trying to cheer you up and order your life around is a pretty grim thought for any child. So there was an obvious beginning and a natural story presented itself in terms of Miranda then deciding she would pull herself together and become 'the new her'. She would do all she could to do this, achieve it, then balls it up and finally realise that people loved her just as she really is. It's a story that is essentially the essence of the show altogether.

A woman struggling against societal pressures to fit in and instead to just be herself and accept herself.

So the question was what to hook this story on comedically. I knew I wanted to trick audiences into thinking that Gary had left for good by getting a new chef in. That way Gary's return would be even more exciting for the audience. But could Miranda really get another good-looking guy? Is that really believable? And cue lots of debate between writers and producers. Rude — I look like Miranda! I think actually, I was the one questioning more than anyone because, well, I look like Miranda. So we had to find a good reason he would be intrigued by this clown of a woman. I also wanted to find a reason to fit the comedy of a bed shop and being mistaken for working in a shop into an episode. So we took being mistaken for working in a shop (which has happened to me, I don't know about you) to the extreme and Miranda ended up hanging out with all the workers having done a four-hour shift. The effect of that scene was that she learnt from the staff she should be stronger on her own and renounce men. The effect of that then (every scene must have its purpose, cause and effect) was that the new chef became intrigued by her.

I also had to find a way to get 'Sushi Restaurant' in this episode. It was on a Post-it note on the office wall and I knew the Miranda character should be funny in a sushi restaurant. It felt ripe for comedy plucking. And possibly good to open the new series with. So one of the things on her list of being the 'new her' was going out to lunch with the girls. And they would do sushi. A lunch scene was of course always going to be funnier if it went wrong and I think we came up with the worst thing that could possibly happen at a sushi conveyor belt. I also knew at the beginning of this series that I had to go for it on the physical side of my performing. Audiences had really seemed to respond to the clowning in the first series, and although comedically I was ready to move on to more relational and emotional stories for the characters, I kind of felt I owed it to the style of the show to do as much as possible physically first. Then I could step away from it a bit.

Next we considered what to do with Penny in this episode. She was going to come to stay with Miranda but she had to be there to serve a purpose so we needed to find ways to either make it worse for Miranda or help her. I did both. Which ended up with her pretending to be a Polish cleaner and cause a mix-up with a goat; and then scrabbling around on the floor to help her daughter at the end of a date. The things I make poor Patricia Hodge do!

All that to give you a small insight into the jigsaw puzzle that is writing a sitcom story. Finding ways to hang the comedy set pieces, making sense of it all, giving purpose to every scene and making sure the characters move forward somehow with each moment. There are a lot of things to intertwine. Excuse me whilst I have a little lie down at the thought. And you can have a read of the script should you wish.

INT. MIRANDA'S SITTING ROOM

Miranda on her sofa, with messy hair and wearing an old fleece.

MIRANDA: (TO CAMERA) Well hello to you my old chums. What a
veritable thrill to see you all again. Particularly you – cheeky.
Now let me get you up to speed. Previously in my life… the gorgeous Gary
upped his sticks to Hong Kong. Which I've been fine about…

*Pulling back to reveal the flat in total disarray, empty wine bottles, pizza boxes, a
pringle packet tower, albums of love songs etc.*

I mean I don't think it's weird making fruit friends. *– bit of mint!
Ollie Orange e.g.*

We reveal a bunch of fruit, dressed up/painted, on the sofa next to her.

I mean things only went wrong when I was with Gary anyway.

EXT. STREET (FLASHBACK)

Gary, Stevie, Clive and Miranda pile out of a cab.

Stevie and Clive head in with going out 'whoops'.

MIRANDA: Oooh, looks great.

*Her wrap-around dress gets stuck in the door and comes off in one swift move-
ment revealing bra and pants.*

She runs after the cab. The others are laughing.

INT. MIRANDA'S SITTING ROOM (BACK TO PRESENT)

MIRANDA: (TO CAMERA) Say nothing. Sshh please. Yeah. No. I'm fine.

Tired, but that's because I've been sleeping on a lilo because my bed broke. Too much action.

INT. MIRANDA'S BEDROOM (FLASHBACK)

Miranda is leaping on her bed to S Club 7's 'Reach For the Stars' and whilst she is bouncing on the bed, Stevie is throwing her sweets to catch. She jumps up and as she lands the bed breaks.

INT. MIRANDA'S SITTING ROOM

MIRANDA: And if I had been down, I definitely turned a corner last night…

INT. CLUB/PUB

Miranda, drunk, doing karaoke in her pyjamas. Singing Daniel Beddingfield's 'If You're Not The One'.

MIRANDA: (SINGING) Is there any way that I can stay in your arms?

It's the really high bit in the song.

SHOUTS ANGRILY: It's too high, Daniel. And unnaturally high for a man.

INT. MIRANDA'S SITTING ROOM. BACK TO PRESENT.

MIRANDA: (TO CAMERA) Right, let's jolly on with the show. Which is filmed in front of a live studio audience. Say hello. THEY DO. See.

OPENING TITLES

I know best without but so want to educate it's in front of audience.
!Aaaah....
AAAAAHHH!

INT. MIRANDA'S SHOP.

Miranda comes downstairs, still wearing tracksuit bottoms, the old fleece with stains on it and her hair is a mess.

The shop has a new upmarket section labelled 'Stevie's Corner'. It sells jewellery and tops/nighties, trinkets and nick-nacks — Oliver Bonas-esque. There's a long mirror.

There are some posh girls looking at the products.

MIRANDA: (DEPRESSED) Hello Stevie.

STEVIE: (DISGUSTED BY HOW SHE LOOKS) Oh dear.

Sprays air freshner

Seeing the posh girls.

MIRANDA: Oh, your new stock keeps bringing in these posh girls…

STEVIE: Sorry are you disparaging Stevie's boutique corner?

MIRANDA: No, maybe. I don't know what disparaging means.

STEVIE: Mocking.

MIRANDA: Oh, then yes.
WITH PRONOUNCED POSH FACE/VOICE: Yup, I'm going to see Hugo, Wills, Milly, Billy and Bella so I need a new trinkety necklace.

She turns around and is face to face with a posh girl.

Hello.

POSH GIRL: Are you making fun of me?

MIRANDA: No, (KEEPS TALKING POSH) no, what do you mean? I mean this is how I speak. So umm… do you need any help at all? (TO CAMERA) It's quite tricky… (TO GIRLS) Anything you'd like to try on?

POSH GIRL: No, we're fine thanks.

STEVIE: Urgh. Have you looked in a mirror recently? Come on, you've got to get your act together, Miranda. Stop wallowing.

MIRANDA: I have stopped wallowing. I've told you I've moved on.

STEVIE: You've stopped thinking about Gary?

MIRANDA: Yes. (TO CAMERA) No.

Too much to camera

STEVIE: You've moved on?

MIRANDA: Yes. (TO CAMERA) No.

STEVIE: You don't think about him?

MIRANDA: No. (TO CAMERA) Yes.

STEVIE: Good. So you won't want to see Gary's postcard that arrived this morning.

Holds it up. Stevie runs round with it.

STEVIE: Ahh! A lovely postcard, written in Gary's lovely fair chef-like hand. The lovely chefy hands of lovely chef Gary.

Miranda chases Stevie. She trips her up so she falls onto beanbag.

MIRANDA: Do you concede?

STEVIE: Yes I concede.

MIRANDA: Thank you. (READING) 'Hey, really enjoying life out here so far. Plans all a bit up in the air. Thinking of you all. Love G.' (BEAT) That's it. After three months he sends me that. Right well, forget him. Seriously.

STEVIE: Good girly.

MIRANDA: Yeah no I will move on. I will be a new me, get fit, lose weight… A new me shall reigneth. Yeah, like a phoenix emerging from the ashes of my old life and flapping off. Behold I am woman. And phoenix. Both. But not in a mutanty way. And yes, I have indeed lost my train of thought.

Tilly struts in.

MIRANDA: Oh no, it's Tilly…

TILLY: Bonjourno peeps. Urgh, Stevie it looks like there's a tramp in the shop. (LAUGHS)

MIRANDA: Where? Where? Uh!

Stevie brings a full length mirror to Miranda, who looks at it and jumps.

The tramp is me.

Thanks Sal. Great Tillyism!

TILLY: You have majorly let yourself go – slackarooni cheese. So Queen Kong I bring good tidings of great joy. Stinky Von Tusse is in town and she wants to luncheon later at the new sushi place. Will you come? It's going to be tremendulant. Aah, Stinky was the most brillo head girl ever. Once (LAUGHS) do you remember? (LAUGHS) She imac-ed a squirrel. (LAUGHS) It was the funniest thing. So will you come, you'll come, you'll come, (MIRANDA TRIES TO ANSWER) no hush, no hush, no hush, no hush, no hush up. You have to come so I don't look like the saddo one in front of Stinkles. OK I am now going to power walk back to the orifice.

pronounce it Tuss but joke is it's the forcep thing in Midwifery – suction thingy

She does a bizarre fast walk out.

Ciao, ciao, ciao, ciao, ciao, ciao. Kapow!

Goes.

STEVIE: You've got to be more assertive, Miranda. What about the new you?

MIRANDA: She'll start on Monday. You always wait till Monday to start a new regime so you can lie about for a few days eating out the fridge convinced on Monday you'll change forever. It's a brilliant system. We all do it.

Too stand-uppy

Starts to go upstairs.

Don't judge me with your little eyes, I've been very depressed. I've been very depressed.

Note to self: find way in rehearsal to button this scene.

She drags herself up the stairs.

INT. MIRANDA'S SITTING ROOM

MIRANDA: Oh look at the state of me, watching telly all day with friends made of fruit, you enjoying it ~~Gail~~? I look like a tramp, got to go to Tilly's lunch, Gary's gone. Suppose it couldn't get worse.

Gordon better? :)

Penny comes in with cases.

PENNY: Darling, I've left your father and I'm coming to live with you.

Miranda cries to camera.

MIRANDA: Oh Mum. Not again?

PENNY: He's bound to crawl back tomorrow – it's nude fondue night.

Miranda grimaces.

Don't worry darling, you won't even notice I'm here.

MIRANDA: (TO CAMERA) Guaranteed I'll be so irritated I'll have to leave in under thirty seconds. Set your watches – go…

PENNY: (FIDDLES WITH MIRANDA'S HAIR) Have you been cutting your own hair?

MIRANDA: Three seconds, already annoyed…

PENNY: And look at all this (RE FLAT MESS)… you should have a bath, then get some air, have a lovely, what I call, walk…

MIRANDA: It is a walk… Mum… Can you…

PENNY: Sorry, won't interfere…

Sits down and watches TV.

MIRANDA: If she calls the remote controls a silly name…

Brief pause.

PENNY: (PICKING UP THREE REMOTES)
You'll have to show me how to work these. I mean who needs
three doobries?

MIRANDA: (GETS UP) Right! That's it! Why's it so annoying?
(TO CAMERA) Twenty seconds. Doobries!

Goes to bedroom.

INT. SHOP

Miranda comes downstairs changed now and looking better.

MIRANDA: So forget Monday, look I'm starting now.

STEVIE: Right then are you ready and happy to speak to Heather?

MIRANDA: Please go ahead.

STEVIE: (SINGS) What have you done today to make you feel proud?

MIRANDA: Well, Heather, Miss Heather Small, hello to you.

STEVIE: Hello!

MIRANDA: Today I have begun the new me.

Stevie claps.

I know Mum and Tilly won't know what's hit them. I'm going to be the kind
of woman… who you know… the kind of woman that just leaps out of bed
and just does that (DEMO) and their hair looks perfect. They then grab a
homemade muffin out of their Cath Kidston polka dot biscuit tin and head

to work, wearing trainers at the bottom of a skirt suit to show off they've power-walked in. They have pot plants that don't die on them. Their fruit bowl isn't full of three week-old rotting pears because they actually eat the fruit. They have day bags, evening bags and a clutch. In their day bags they have a particular pouch for their mobile so when it rings – bam, they're there. They know about and have an interest in pelmets. You know, they just grab a wheatgerm smoothie in between work because that's enough to keep them going, even though at lunch time they jogged – and enjoyed it, because they don't have flesh that moves independently to their main frame. And finally they have easy access to pens to finish a crossword at a bar where the man they decided to take as a lover the night before says to them 'Hey, last night was great'. (BEAT) You know I'll be that kind of woman.

Good luck me learning that speech!

STEVIE: Yeah, well good luck with that.

PENNY: Darling, I'm putting on a whites wash, if your pants are dirty, pop them off, I'll pop them in… (GOES)

MIRANDA: Right, well, that's not the best of starts, she'll have to go. But don't worry the new me shall still reigneith.

She starts pacing femininely.

Yeah, look at her forming before your very eyes.

She puts on a piece of jewellery.

Now excuse me, I'm off to have sushi with Tilly and Stinky in my new (POSHLY) trinkety necklace.

Miranda leaves

Do the same as Tilly did in the last
shop scene:- Ciao, ciao, ciao etc…

INT. SUSHI BAR

Miranda, Stinky and Tilly are in a row at the conveyor belt.
They are doing a crossword.

STINKY: Eight down, 'Remove vehicles, reversing at back of depot'. Oh well… that could be van… lorry…

MIRANDA: Yep, hang on, I know this… I can so get this… It's umm…

STINKY: Subtract, of course. Right, let's eat. It all looks edible von guzzle bucket.

TILLY: I'm starvington stations.

MIRANDA: Yup, Hungelos McMungelos.

Tilly and Stinky start eating. Miranda tries to pick some food up with chopsticks, drops it just before getting it in her mouth. Spits it out.

TILLY: Stinky do you remember the time that I got locked in the boot... (GETS TEXT) Sorry. Oh, bear with, bear with, bear... Ooh fabulasmic VIP invite to a scoffulate dans le city avec de rien de sleepage.

During their conversation they continue eating, Miranda struggling with the food.

STINKY: So Queen Kong, what news with you?

MIRANDA: Oh well, I'm just focussing on my business at the moment. We do trinkets and nick-nacks now – this is one of ours...

STINKY: Gorge, and are we lucksville in love?

Tilly laughs.

MIRANDA: Actually I did get a postcard from an old beau, Gary, this morning... so yeah (GETS A TEXT) Ooh, ooh. Bear with, bear with, bear with... (SHE RIFLES IN HER BAG TO FIND HER PHONE) (READS IT OUT CONFIDENTLY) Call now for a new tariff breakdown...

TILLY: (READING THE POSTCARD) Oh dear. Sounds like you might have lost him to his travels...

MIRANDA: Oh well that's fine if I have, I'm so over him. I'm a whole new...

Miranda goes to grab the postcard, Stinky takes it off Tilly. Miranda leans further to get it but in doing so falls on to the conveyor belt. Her necklace gets caught in it and she starts being dragged around by it.

No I'm stuck. My trinkety necklace.

TILLY: Undo it at the back.

MIRANDA: I can't. I'm going to have to get on. Sorry about this… sorry everyone, so sorry.

Possibly pass a couple at conveyor: hello how are you?! To waitress: I will have to mount your travelator.

Could do a riff on 'not mount in that way'

✗ too much

STINKY: Oh Queen Kong you're such a dweeb.

She manages to unhook herself.

MIRANDA: I've unhooked. I've unhooked. Sorry about this, sorry. I'll just finish the circuit. Saves walking.

STINKY: Utterly mortifying.

MIRANDA: Sorry.

She gets back and slides cooly off the conveyor.

Maybe add Soy sauce to people when they pass "whilst I'm here."

MIRANDA: Where were we?

STINKY: Leaving.

The restaurant owner comes out. People point to Miranda who ducks.

MIRANDA: Quick…

They leave.

INT. RESTAURANT

The girls are at a table. Clive is taking the orders.

STINKY: I could woof a gateaux, but just a peppermint tea for me.

TILLY: Yup could absolutely scoffulate a puddington, but just a skinny cap please.

MIRANDA: Oh yeah, I could inhale a meal-y-von-neely, but just a crumble please. With just cream and just custard and just ice cream.

CLIVE: Are you still feeling bad about Gary?

MIRANDA: Can people stop asking me that? I'm fine.

CLIVE: Good because there's a new chef arriving any minute…
I was gonna tell you…

MIRANDA: Really? Well actually, that's good. Now I know Gary's not coming back. Yeah that's good, gone are the days where I pathetically make an idiot of myself over some hunky chef.

The restaurant door opens.

CLIVE: This must be him…

The new chef (Danny) walks in. He is in bike leathers with helmet on.

We hear the Top Gun *theme.*

He comes up to them, takes his bike helmet off. He is tall and good looking.

Miranda clocks camera with an 'oh no'.

The girls just stare.

MIRANDA: Clive, can you switch that music off please?

CLIVE: Sorry.

We see Clive by the CD machine. He switches Top Gun *music off.*

DANNY: Hi. Clive is it?

CLIVE: Yes, nice to meet you at last.

The girls are all staring.

DANNY: (TO THE GIRLS) Hi girls.

Tilly and Stinky stand, followed by Miranda.

TILLY / STINKY: Hola.

MIRANDA: Hello. (SHE STARTS CURTSEYING)
(TO CAMERA) Why am I curtseying. I've just got to keep going now.
(TO DANNY) How do you do?

She gets up and as she does so she farts.

Sorry sorry. That was my dog.

DANNY: What was?

MIRANDA: That noise.

DANNY: I thought that was a chair scraping?

MIRANDA: Oh it was.

DANNY: Then what was your dog?

MIRANDA: I don't have a dog.

DANNY: You said the noise was your dog?

MIRANDA: Well it might have been YOUR dog.

DANNY: I don't have a dog.

MIRANDA: Well can you stop saying you do.

Miranda clocks camera.

Curtseying should be a running theme in series

CLIVE: Right, so everyone, this is Danny…

DANNY: (SINGING) I got chills, they're multi-plying… And I'm losing control…

They all stare at him with – 'wow'!

(WITH PRIDE) Always get Danny from *Grease* with the bike leathers, the accent…

GIRLS: (SINGING) You better shape up coz I need a man, and my heart is set on you…

Laughs.

MIRANDA: You're the one that I want, you're the one I want… We've stopped.

Tilly/Stinky sit down.

(OFF AGAIN)The one I need, oh yes indeed. Sorry, it's a sort of weirdly hard tune to stop. (SINGING AGAIN) You're the one that I want… I'm off again. Ooh, ooh, ooh honey.

They all stare.

Look, there's a thing…

Points in one direction.

She runs really fast out in other direction.

INT. SHOP

Miranda comes in.

Stevie is at the till.

MIRANDA: Stevie, Stevie, Stevie, Stevie, Stevie, Stevie, Stevie, Stevie… I'm with much news, which I shall now birth.

STEVIE: Ready to receive caller.

MIRANDA: A new chef has arrived at the restaurant who you could happily compare to some kind of God, and he would very much be in the running for the new me to take as her lover… but the new me is currently worse than the old me…

STEVIE: This is not possible.

MIRANDA: I farted in front of him, blamed it on an imaginary dog and sung in his face. I give up.

STEVIE: Maybe you should try that life coach again.

MIRANDA: No thanks.

INT. HALL (FLASHBACK)

A group of people doing a session with a life coach, including Stevie. They are all blowing up balloons.

Mel Giedroyc be great

LIFE COACH: Imagine your anxieties filling the balloon.

We reveal Miranda with a massive balloon or bin bag.

Suddenly it pops. She screams.

MIRANDA: (STRESSED) Oh no, my anxieties are everywhere…
save yourselves…

Cut to:

INT. SHOP. BACK TO PRESENT

Penny comes in carrying a mop, and a few carrier bags.

PENNY: Right, I'm going to start a spring clean, even though it is, what
I call, November. And are you going to get a new bed? We can't both
sleep on the lilo.

MIRANDA: (POINTEDLY) Well maybe one of us should leave.

PENNY: Where would you go? (BEAT) Don't worry if Nude Fondue doesn't
make your father want me back, he'll be desperate for my
Kinky Quiche.

MIRANDA: (TO CAMERA) Yuck.

PENNY: Do you want me to get you a bed?

MIRANDA: No, I'll get my own bed thank you.

PENNY: Don't forget your keys…

MIRANDA: (AS TEENAGER) I'm not six. (LEAVES) (BEAT) (COMES IN)
I forgot my keys…

Penny smiles and goes upstairs. Miranda points angrily at Penny.

STEVIE: Don't panic, we'll force her out, now what does she hate?

Miranda grabs a lolly from till area to eat.

MIRANDA: I don't know, I'm too depressed to think straight. (WHILST
EATING) Ghosts, she hates ghosts. But how's that gonna work?

She walks slowly out then sinks to the floor and drags herself out.

Don't worry about me. I'll just be fine, I'll just…

INT. BED SHOP

Miranda is lying on a bed. There is a tea tray display on the bedside table.

79

MIRANDA: Mmm yeah, this is nice. Although if you eat in bed you can get the nasty condition, crumb bed. You lie down and feel the abrasive itch of a crumb. Horrid, you have to get it out. And you don't want to miss a crumb so you can't go too big on the crumb bed manoeuvre.

Ryan, shop assistant, approaches.

Miranda stops and gets out.

RYAN: If you like the bed, there's an offer, free duvet - it's fifteen tog.

MIRANDA: Tog. It's a funny word isn't it.

RYAN: Yes, suppose it is. (LAUGHS MANICALLY. BIZARRE LAUGH)

Miranda looks startled.

She sees a single bunk bed with a slide attached.

MIRANDA: Right, oh those look fun. All you'd need would be a ball pool to land in for mornings to be a total joy.

RYAN: Ball pool. (LAUGHS)

Miranda looks startled, brief glance to camera.

Yeah, they're great for kids.

MIRANDA: Yes, no I wasn't thinking for me. (TO CAMERA) I was, I was. (RE ANOTHER BED). Ooh. This is a nice one.

RYAN: Try it. I've just got to see to this gentleman. It's got a lovely ridged frame. The bed not the gentleman. (THE LAUGH)

He touches Miranda's arm, she bats it away.

MIRANDA: Get off!

WOMAN: Excuse me, could you tell me what tog these duvets are?

MIRANDA: Oh umm... I don't... Well, they're fifteen tog.

*Costume note
make sure my
outfit is like
what staff at
shop will wear.*

WOMAN: And do the beds come ready assembled?

MIRANDA: I have no idea. Can you stop asking me questions.

WOMAN: Well there's no need for that attitude. Excuse me are you
the manager...?

To the boss who walks past.

This woman has been quite rude...

MIRANDA: I'm not being quite rude.

BOSS: Don't argue with the customer. You must be the new girl. (TO WOMAN) I'm so sorry madam, I'll sort this out myself.

Woman goes.

Right you, now where's your name badge?

Picks up the remaining name badge from a box labelled 'staff badges' on a table. Gives it to Miranda. It reads Sandy.

Here you are, this must be you – now I need…

MIRANDA: The thing is…

BOSS: Do not argue back, I need you down the warehouse now, we're completely over-stretched.

Moves off.

MIRANDA: But…

BOSS: (SHOUTING) C'mon hurry up…

Miranda hurries along and clocks camera.

INT. BED SHOP WAREHOUSE

Miranda is driving a fork-lift carrying some beds. CAN'T WAIT!

MIRANDA: (TO CAMERA) I think this has got a bit out of hand.

INT. BED SHOP STAFF ROOM

A group of staff having a tea break. Michelle (ballsy, Essex girl)
is making cups of tea.

MICHELLE: So have you got a boyfriend, Sandy?

MIRANDA: (CHECKS HER NAME BADGE) Sandy, that's me. I dunno —
does Sandy have a boyfriend? Well I'd know wouldn't I, being Sandy. Does
Sandy have a boyfriend, no she doesn't. (LAUGHS)

MICHELLE: Good. Coz we were all sayin' yesterday — we should like totally
renounce men. Do you know what I'm saying?

MIRANDA: I do know what you're saying, yeah that sounds great. Yeah.
(TO CAMERA) I've caught her accent. (TO MICHELLE) Renouncing men —
yeah bring it on my sisters.

MICHELLE: Yeah, coz we don't need males. In' that right?

MIRANDA: Innit just right though innit. (LOOKS TO CAMERA) You know, I've had enough of men. Innit?

Hope this doesn't feel too done, comedy wise

MICHELLE: That's it… go girl…

MIRANDA: Oh do you want me to go? Oh I see. Sorry, you go girl. Yeah, no, I go. Exactly, go me, go Sandy. Yeah, I'm saying to myself this, Sandy, I'm saying, Sandy, I was saying to myself, you my girl, will not be pushed around no more.

MICHELLE: Do you know what I mean?

MIRANDA: Well I do yes because I just said it.

Ryan comes in

What are you doing back here?

MIRANDA: I'm Sandy…

RYAN: No you're not.

MIRANDA: Says who?

RYAN: I do.

MIRANDA: Oh do you now do you do diddly do?
(TO CAMERA) Gone Irish.

RYAN: I think you should leave.

MIRANDA: Not before I show you the bed I want, and at a staff discount... Never let them push you around girls, yeah?

MICHELLE: Do you get me?

MIRANDA: Go me. Go Sandy.

The girls all whoop. Miranda does some dance groove out.

INT. SHOP

Miranda comes swaggering confidently in to the shop.

STEVIE: And where have you been?

MIRANDA: I did a four-hour shift at the bed shop. But more importantly have I discovered my inner Sandy. Yo girlfriend.

They shake hands.

STEVIE: I already like Sandy...

MIRANDA: Yeah she's wicked. And Sandy says, well I say, we both say, we are one and the same... briefly having an existential crisis... We, I, am renouncing men... Coz here's the thing. Come here – (THEY HUDDLE). We could get any man if we wanted to. And she said , well I say, we/I am renouncing men. Yeah are you with me, I'm renouncing men. Amen.

STEVIE: Course we could, look at us.

MIRANDA: And what I slash Sandy says is this, wait for it, (DRAMATICALLY) I am my own husband.

STEVIE: Oh, I like that.

MIRANDA: It's good isn't it? In a nutshell — I'm practical enough to change a lightbulb, but I get the bed to myself. You with me?

Danny comes in. Miranda has back to door.

STEVIE: A man.

Miranda does a turn/jumps at Danny.

MIRANDA: A man. Sorry — I see. A man. (BEAT) Hello.

DANNY: Hi. Clive said you worked here? Nice shop.

MIRANDA: Thanks. Do you like my trinkets? Not a euphemism.

She struts to the till and clocks camera.

DANNY: I'm looking for someone to show me around. Clive also said you're the only single lady in town.

STEVIE: I'm also sing…

Miranda pushes her off her stool.

MIRANDA: Yeah that's me.

DANNY: Is that because you're renouncing men?

MIRANDA: Ah yes, yup…

DANNY: OK. That's a shame.

Starts to go.

STEVIE: (WHISPERING) What are you doing? You can't renounce him!

MIRANDA: (WHISPERING) Well I can't suddenly un-renounce, he'll think I'm odd and confused. Which I am but we must hide this.

STEVIE: Sandy isn't odd and confused – go get your Danny.

MIRANDA/STEVIE: Oohh Sandy and Danny…

STEVIE: And if you don't go for it, then I'll whip out my allure…

Danny has walked back from the door. Suddenly they see him there and jump.

DANNY: Now, I don't like getting a no.

STEVIE: (FLIRTING) Oh well I'd say yes.

Miranda pushes her off her stool again.

DANNY: Are you renouncing all men? What if I asked you out tonight…

MIRANDA: Well, I would say, that you are officially renounced… but…

She moves around to sit sexily on the edge of the till.

(TO CAMERA) This better look good, because I'm sitting on something very uncomfortable. ⎯⎯ *Too graphic?!*

There's a clause in my renouncement that says… this – if somebody is new to an area, and asks a woman out on their first night, the aforementioned woman mentioned heretofore is obliged nay commanded nay must accept.

DANNY: That's a good clause. I like a headstrong independent woman.

MIRANDA: Well hello.

DANNY: My last girlfriend lived with her mum. Pretty freaky huh?

PENNY: (COMING DOWNSTAIRS) Miranda, I've washed your control pants. (HOLDING THEM UP) That should suck it all back in.

MIRANDA: This is my cleaner...

PENNY: Well excuse me...

MIRANDA: (TO PENNY, WHISPERED) He's asking me out...

PENNY: (IN A KIND OF POLISH ACCENT) Well hello, I am cleaner. Miss Penelopia...

STEVIE: Where are you from?

PENNY: (IN ACCENT) Poland? (BEAT) And I was coming down because I needed polish. Imagine. I am Polish, and I forgot my polish. (LAUGHS)

DANNY: OK, I'll see you later. (LEAVING) six-thirty?

MIRANDA: Lovely.

He leaves.

They should all curtsey!

Mum, make sure you're out of the flat tonight.

PENNY: Why because he might come back? (LAUGHS)

Stevie laughs. Stevie and Penny high five.

MIRANDA: He might. He might. (TO CAMERA) He might.

INT. MIRANDA'S SITTING ROOM

Miranda comes out of her bedroom changed into a dress for her date.

She is trying to get her tights on.

The flat is looking a lot cleaner… but still a bit messy, stuff lying about.

Stevie is helping Miranda get ready – brushing her hair, spraying scent. There is a general fuss.

There is also a goat on the sofa!

STEVIE: Hurry up, he is downstairs. Can't believe you slept all afternoon.

MIRANDA: I know, I just meant to try my new bed…

Re tights palava: "ONE SIZE DOES NOT FIT ALL!"

Miranda suddenly sees the goat. Stares at it, and stares at camera.

STEVIE: Oh yes, I forgot to say.

MIRANDA: There's a massive goat in my sitting room and you just forgot to say.

STEVIE: It's good isn't it?

Miranda looks confused.

You said your mum hates goats.

MIRANDA: GHOSTS. I said GHOSTS. Who has any strong opinions on goats?

STEVIE: I did think it was odd.

MIRANDA: And you didn't think to check before, how…?

Penny enters carrying some shopping, starts unpacking. Including a house plant and fruit.

PENNY: Don't worry, I'm going out, I've just bought a few more things to spruce…

Suddenly sees the goat and stares.

STEVIE: Ooh scary isn't it? Grrr a goat.

DANNY: (OOV) Hello?

MIRANDA: Quick!

Moving Penny out of the way sprays perfume.

Miranda pushes her to the bedroom.

Danny appears at the door.

DANNY: Hi?

MIRANDA: Hello.

Miranda dives to the doorway to lean in it so he can't come in.

DANNY: You all ready?

MIRANDA: Yes um, Let me just grab my clutch… clutch bag…

Stevie passes it.

Good word: clutch, isn't it. Clutch.

Suddenly the goat bleats

DANNY: What was that?

MIRANDA: (BLEATS) Me, I'm just so excited. (BLEATS) So shall we go?

She rushes out, indicating to Stevie to get rid of the goat.

INT. MIRANDA'S FLAT

Maybe they could sing "tell me more" from Grease

Miranda and Danny come through the door laughing.

The flat looks amazing, really tidy, plants, cookie jars, a bowl of fruit, home made biscuits.

DANNY: Wow, what a beautiful place…

MIRANDA:

Sees it.

Wow.

DANNY: Can I use your loo?

He takes a biscuit.

MIRANDA: Yeah help yourself.

MIRANDA: Yes sure it's through there…

DANNY: Did you make these?

Miranda nods.

DANNY: (TRYING A BISCUIT)
What do you use?

On way to bathroom.

MIRANDA: Umm… Flour, food, hobs… nobs…

PENNY: (WHISPERS FROM BEHIND THE SOFA)
Nutmeg…

MIRANDA: Nutmeg.

Looks around and screams on seeing Penny.

I'm a nut for nutmeg.

He goes to bathroom.

(WHISPERS) Mum, what are you doing here?

PENNY: Sorry. I didn't think he'd come back and your father's changed the locks…

MIRANDA: I'm not interested. Quick, get in the bedroom.

Miranda is bustling Penny to the bedroom.

Loo flushes, and door opens, Miranda hides Penny behind the armchair.

MIRANDA: Ah hello, do you want to take a seat?

Miranda ushers him to the sofa.

Err, a drink?

DANNY: A scotch if you have one… I have to say I think I got you all wrong.

Miranda goes to the kitchen. We see Penny crawl over to Miranda.

PENNY: (WHISPERING) Use the nice tumblers.

DANNY: What?

MIRANDA: Use the nice tumblers… I said to myself…
(MOUTHS TO PENNY) get out…

Returns with a glass.

There you go.

DANNY: Thanks…

Worried about this scene – timing gotta be perf. Eek.

RELAX

94

They sit down. He downs his drink.

I'm glad you came out tonight…

MIRANDA: Yes me too.

He turns to put his drink down/perhaps look at a photo or something.

Penny starts styling Miranda's hair.

Miranda bats her away. Danny turns back.

Penny ducks and Miranda turns it into sexy hair tossing.

One doesn't always feel in the mood to renounce… hence the unrenouncement clause. You know.

Miranda looks worried as she sees Penny filling up Danny's glass behind him.

DANNY: Could I get another scotch…

MIRANDA: There you go…

He turns and sees it's full.

DANNY: Wow. You seem to have everything under control. It's very sexy.

Danny leans in for a kiss.

Suddenly we see Penny popping her head up from behind him, giving Miranda the thumbs up.

MIRANDA: (GETTING UP) Sorry, I'm gonna have to stop you there…

DANNY: Oh, that's disappointing.

Gets up.

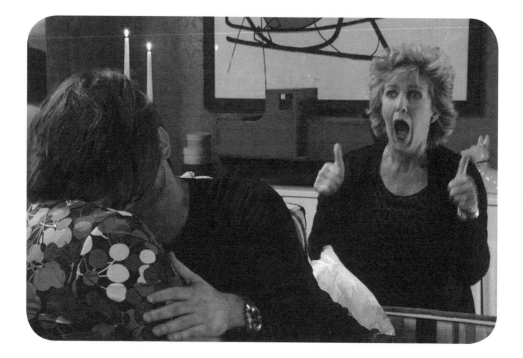

You're quite something…

MIRANDA: So they say.

DANNY: Can I call you?

MIRANDA: Sure you've got my number. Ciao!

He goes. She shuts the door. Penny pops up.

MIRANDA: He is in my palm.

They both start moving excitedly.

INT. MIRANDA'S FLAT

Dolly Parton's '9 to 5' is on. To 'Tumbled out of bed and a stumble to the kitchen'.
Miranda comes out of her room.

can't clear the track to use on Tv. Go with:- Raining Men

She pauses in the door frame and flicks her hair.

She has a skirt and a shirt on and a belt around her waist with trainers looking the businesswoman.

She bops/moves to the music whilst she takes a gulp of orange juice, grabs a cookie from the polka dot cookie jar, waters her plant, sees a pen on the table, puts it in her shirt pocket.

We also see a bowl of fruit. She grabs a handbag, and heads out…

EXT. STREET

Struts

She walks along, passing the other posh girls from earlier in skirts and trainers. They nod to her.

INT. RESTAURANT

The montage continues.

Miranda walks in, sits elegantly on a stool.

Clive is doing a crossword…

CLIVE: To mock or belittle, nine letters.

MIRANDA: Disparage.

He is looking for a pen. She hands him one.

CLIVE: Who are you?

Danny appears.

DANNY: Hey, last night was great…

Miranda realises she has achieved her aim.
She looks excitedly to camera.

MIRANDA: (TO CAMERA) I did it.

We reveal Tilly and Stinky having breakfast, staring at her, amazed.

MIRANDA: Not so much a dweeb now.

DANNY: Although there is one thing that was missing…

He kisses her and… Gary walks in.

GIRLS: Gary!

GARY: Hi.

Miranda turns to see him. She looks shocked.

Then falls off her stool. Grabs for a table, manages only to pull the table cloth off, sends food everywhere.

MIRANDA: Hello.

INT. SHOP

Miranda is in a state, pacing. Stevie and Clive are following her closely around.

MIRANDA: Gary sent the postcard after he got there but it only just arrived.

She stops, Stevie and Clive bang in to her.

STEVIE/CLIVE: Sorry.

MIRANDA: And now feel a bit teary actually because I've been thinking about him for months you know, why is he suddenly back?

They all give her a hug.

CLIVE: I think he said he got the sack.

MIRANDA: Really?

STEVIE: We need to find out his situation.

MIRANDA: Yeah but what do I do about…

Danny, Gary come in.

DANNY: Listen, I've been let go. Gary's contract's still open.

STEVIE/CLIVE: Gary's got his job back. ——— *whisper like school kids. Grease-esque!*

99

GARY: But if I'm staying then, I don't want this to be awkward…

MIRANDA: Awkward? This? Awkward.

Struggling to stand naturally.

MIRANDA: Who's awkward? Funny word awkward. Something awkward about the word awkward. (SUDDENLY) Clutch. No sorry I'm cas…

Stands to demonstrate.

STEVIE: (QUICKLY, HUSHED) You're acting weird. Look, ask if Gary's got a girlfriend.

MIRANDA: Gary, so what does your girlfriend think of you leaving Hong Kong?

GARY: I don't have a girlfriend…

STEVIE/CLIVE: ~~Doesn't have a girlfriend.~~

DANNY: So, Gary was telling me about this job in Birmingham. I might check it out if that's cool…

MIRANDA: (TO DANNY) Of course… I mean this… this was only…

STEVIE: (REALLY QUICKLY SO MIRANDA MIGHT HARDLY HEAR) Ask if Gary's considered the job in Birmingham?

MIRANDA: Have you considered the joggers, that you might burn in them?

STEVIE/CLIVE: Backfired. Backfired.

DANNY: I better go, I've got a hunch that I might have got in the middle of something here…

MIRANDA/GARY: (PASSING IT OFF) What? Us? No, no we're just friends… nothing here, he/I just got back from Hong Kong.

Stevie and Clive look at each other. It's obvious there is something.

DANNY: Right, goodbye.

He kisses her and goes.

GARY: So, things have changed a bit.

MIRANDA: Yep it's just the new me.

Stevie/Clive give her the thumbs up.

Then Penny comes downstairs.

PENNY: Miranda, I think that goat ate your bunion insole. (HOLDS IT UP)

The sushi owner and a policeman come in.

POLICEMAN: Excuse me, we need to talk about the damage to this man's restaurant.

RYAN: (RUSHING IN) That's her.

SANDY: I'm Sandy, stop impersonating me or I'll report you.

DELIVERY GUY: (COMING IN) Kids ball pool for Miranda?

MIRANDA: Welcome back.

GARY: I think I preferred the old you anyway. Come here.

They hug.

STEVIE: Ball pool?

MIRANDA: Yes, follow me.

They all go upstairs.

Dolly Parton's 9-5' plays.

IT'S RAINING MEN

INT. MIRANDA'S BEDROOM

We reveal Miranda's new bed — it's the bunk with a slide.

The cast all slide down in to the ball pool one by one. (N.B. If that takes too long, everyone could be in and on different part of the bed for the reveal and their waves.)

You have been watching

Miranda Hart

Sarah Hadland

Patricia Hodge

James Holmes

Tom Ellis —

maybe he could
pop up from
under duvet in
bed: Subtext!

Michael Landes. Waves as he heads out of the restaurant.

Sally Phillipps and Belinda Stewart-Wilson in the restaurant, Belinda waves and follows Danny out.

We cut back to the cast dancing in the bedroom/ball pool.

Series Two, Episode One
Behind the Scenes Tit-Bits

🎬 One of my favourite scenes out of all the series to rehearse, and then perform on the night of recording, was when the replacement chef comes in and the girls sing 'You're The One That I Want' from Grease and then I do a fart and blame it on an imaginary dog. We all got the giggles the first time we read it but I think possibly I was the only one still laughing on day three of rehearsals. On the night the fart got such a huge laugh – we genuinely think the audience thought I had actually farted.

🎬 We auditioned a variety of 15 fart sounds. Fact.

🎬 I really hurt my knee doing the sushi belt stunt. I basically had to actually do it for real as the necklace had to be stuck down to make it look realistic. And clambering on to a high sushi belt wasn't easy time and time again.

🎬 The goat did a massive and very loud wee before, during and after every take of that scene.

🎬 Sarah Hadland became obsessed with the goat. It was her favourite co-star. Rude. Second favourite the Chihuahua in Series One, Episode Six.

I now regularly get sent fruit friends. I had no idea one silly joke at the beginning of this episode would become a thing.

In rehearsals I kept forgetting the long speech I had about turning into the New Me so Sarah put lots of sticky notes on the counter of the joke shop with things like 'pear' and 'mobile phone' on them in case I forgot on the night in front of the audience. She was pretending to write out price tags for shop items but she was actually writing down prompts.

Tom Ellis was really nervous about coming back in at the end of this episode in case the audience didn't react and wanted the new chef to stay instead of Gary returning. Bless him!

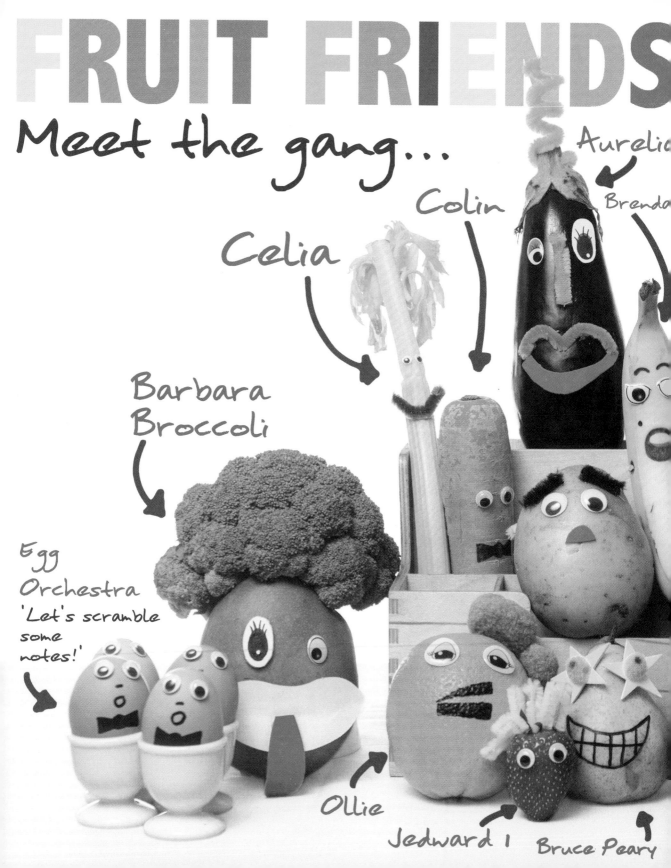

& VEGETAPALS

Perry

Carly

Alice

Gordon

Mr Butternut

Marj

The Beauty Teapot

Tommy

Jedward 2

'I'm a little coconut'

Stunts and Falls

I have been loathe to talk about the falls and stunts in the show because I get defensive that actually they make up entirely about five minutes of the nine hours of material I have written. However, I am pleased that people warmed to the physical side of the show and I am proud about how we executed some of them. My three favourites are...

The Taxi...

Series Two, Episode One

his wasn't a stunt as such, but a big physical set piece that needed to work in one smooth
movement so it took (unfortunately — I am not a massive fan of running up and down a London
treet in just bra and pants, call me old fashioned) quite a few takes to get it right. Sometimes the
ress wouldn't rip fully off. Sometimes the taxi sped away too quickly. There were a lot of things that
ould go wrong in the timing. And it is all done in one shot. Usually I knew it hadn't quite worked
nd wouldn't run too far after the taxi, but the shot we used, I knew it felt right so kept on running. I
ouldn't hear anyone shout cut so carried on for quite a way, before turning around and seeing the
ntire crew laughing.

The Grave...

I know comedically other people have fallen in a grave before, but I don't think anyone else has done it having just said "I was mortified, I wish the ground could swallow me up". That got me really excited and I knew I had to do it. Even though it involved our props guys actually digging a grave in a grave site. It felt a bit morbid for a piece of clowning. On the day I got nervous for the first time before a stunt. Usually I just fall to the ground. And I can do that even just on carpet in front of the live audience. But suddenly I was falling in to a hole, so I was falling four or five feet below ground level to ensure clearing it so you never saw a foot or my back or anything. It was a little intimidating. The grave was padded out with crash mats but still it was a long way to fall. We did it twice and although it was quite funny, on watching it back I knew I had to just keep looking ahead. I used to turn to Penny when I said the line – a natural instinct but also I think because then I could take a sneak peek at where I was going to fall. But I had to do it a third time. I just wanted to look ahead and trust. I knew it would be funnier. Everyone was a little nervous for me doing it again, but I was certain. And that was the take that you'll see. I am glad I only had to do it three times

The Gate...

Series Three, Episode Three

I liked this one because it had the biggest context and justification for a piece of physical comedy. Miranda was really trying to impress her boyfriend, she was feeling confident and happy in herself and then it wasn't her fault, it was just bad luck that the gate started falling backwards. And then I liked the fact that for once after a fall, the person didn't notice. She pulled off the elegant girlfriend. So for that context this may nudge to number 1. But comedically I would say the grave was my number 1. Although much harder to do, the gate was actually fun. I was happy to do it the four or five times I had to. I fell on to two large crash mats on my back and didn't feel too concerned about sustaining an injury. And it was a beautiful sunny day in Gunnesbury Park, West London. The only thing I was nervous about was the two fabulous prop guys who had control of the gate on a large bit of rope — we had to work out how fast they pulled the gate back and I was worried that they might once really yank it so that I fell properly. Just for their own amusement!

A New Low

. . .

I slightly made a rod for my own back with this episode as I chucked so many different strands at it. I think it was one of the first episodes I wrote for Series Two, I will think of the general arc for the series as regards Miranda and Gary but other than that it's an episodic series so I don't necessarily write them in order. So, I had the 'audience member hovering over the remote control' image as more of a threat than ever on this one as it was the first I wrote for the tricky second album. Plus, the difficulty of a studio audience sitcom is that, well beyond simply treating you as if you are total idiots, you have to make the audience laugh. You need gags, you need big laughs. So any emotional stories, any pathos, anything with nuance like the Miranda and Gary through line has to be punctuated with laughter and kept light. It would be much easier to just focus on the drama of their relationship.

So having come up with the Miranda and Gary storyline for this episode I was worried it was a bit too dramatic or 'soapy'. In fact, discovering Gary had been married before really did feel like a soap story. But we knew we needed something as big as that because the audience had to believe why Miranda would step away from him. Otherwise people might be shouting at their TV screens, 'Oh just get together for heaven's sake'. And I never wanted that. There has to be a very good reason to keep them apart. So with this 'soap' I needed a big comedy storyline to go alongside it.

I had always wanted to do a story about keeping up with a 22-year-old. It felt like an identifiable theme to most people over the age of, well, 23. Certainly anyone over 35, when clubbing starts to become a thing of a past and slippers and early nights a highlight. So when the 22-year-old being married to Gary idea came together, then we had a sitcom story. We could hang the Gary and Miranda thread on this comic concept, which became more of a comedic story when I made it a competition between Miranda and Stevie. First against each other and then together against the 22-year-old.

But with the image of the viewer with their remote control still looming, that didn't seem enough to me. I had to make it really hard for myself and add in a story about Miranda not coping with nudity. That then justified the set piece of a life drawing class, and the hideousness of a communal swimming pool changing room, plus it tied in with Miranda and Gary getting together. But I decided that still wasn't enough. I wanted to add in more of a character trait for Gary and brought in the alpha male builder that he tried to compete with. So there were now four to five stories in the one episode. I could have perhaps taken two of these and given them more time to breathe and got two shows out of the ideas, however I wanted to pack each episode with as much as possible. Even though it became incredibly difficult to piece together and tighten down to the best bits of each scene. But I am pleased with how it turned out. It's very busy and fast, but I think it's clear. And if you like my comedy shizzle, I think I can be brave in saying that I don't think you'd press the remote on this episode.

INT. MIRANDA'S SITTING ROOM (MORNING)

Miranda on her sofa.

MIRANDA: (TO CAMERA) Well hello to you. Now come on settle down, you coming in with your cup of tea, you're late. I mean obviously I can't see you but if you were coming in with a cup of tea then, spooky slash exciting moment. So, previously in my life, it became obvious why I have an element of the prude about me.

INT. PENNY'S SITTING ROOM (FLASHBACK. NIGHT)

Miranda walks into the sitting room.

MIRANDA: Mum? Dad? Listen I was wondering if I could borrow…

She opens a door to look for them and screams.

Urh, urh, oh my eyes…

PENNY: (OOV) Sorry darling, Tuesday nights are now naughty knitting night. Such fun.

MIRANDA: Not fun.

INT. MIRANDA'S SITING ROOM (MORNING)

Back to present

MIRANDA: (TO CAMERA) What else? Oh yes, I've got a new friend. Tamara – she's waitressing at the restaurant. She's only twenty-two – but I keep up pretty well… oh yeah.

Cut to:

EXT. PARK (FLASHBACK)

Miranda and Tamara are having a picnic.

MIRANDA: Oh Tamara, I think you've put a sausage roll in the scotch egg tub. Doesn't matter. Go with the flow.

TAMARA: Hey, let's roll down here. (POINTING TO A HILL)

MIRANDA: Right OK, crazy. The mind of the youth.

Tamara rolls down.

Miranda rolls.

I don't like it, I don't. Why would you do that?

INT. MIRANDA'S SITTING ROOM

Back to present.

MIRANDA: (TO CAMERA) And Gary and I haven't talked since he said we should have (MOUTHED) sex. I'm not bothered because I have a very fulfilling and exciting home life. Last night was crazy…

INT. MIRANDA'S BATHROOM (FLASHBACK)

Miranda gets the shower hose, lays it in the bath. Gets herself ready and excited.

Switches the tap on.

The shower hose goes crazy in the bath, like they do, spraying water everywhere.

Miranda is screaming with excitement.

Thank goodness this actually happened at home a few nights ago. !Comedy God exists!

INT. MIRANDA'S FLAT

Back to present.

MIRANDA: (TO CAMERA) See. Good times. Right, let's jolly on with the show.

TITLE SEQUENCE

INT. SHOP

Miranda comes downstairs. Stevie is cowering behind the till.

MIRANDA: What are you doing?

Stevie points to other end of the shop.

MIRANDA: Youths.

We see some teenagers looking at products/laughing.

She hides behind the till with Stevie. They whisper.

Look at them, they're like a pack of shell-suited hyenas.

STEVIE: Hyenae.

MIRANDA: Hyenae. I bet they don't even care about Latin plurals.

STEVIE: Well don't start speaking in Latin plurals.

MIRANDA: I won't. I hope not to engage with them at all.

They start approaching

MIRANDA / STEVIE: Ooh no.

STEVIE: Right don't let them smell our fear. Act casual.

They start whistling Archers theme tune maybe.

TEENAGER: Let me get this innit.

Puts a product down and mumbles a sentence.

Do you get me?

MIRANDA / STEVIE: Absolutely, yeah, totally.

Teenager puts money down.

TEENAGER: I like your mask (POINTING AT MIRANDA'S FACE).
Is it a Halloween one?

Happened to me – Londis, Fulham 2007!

He high fives his mates. Miranda and Stevie do fake laughing.

More mumbles.

Do you know what I mean?

MIRANDA: Yes. (TO CAMERA) No.

They go.

Phew.

STEVIE: How pathetic. You know, we are grown women.

MIRANDA: Well one of us has grown. Tiny! Right, I'm off to the restaurant.

STEVIE: (CHILDISHLY, LIKE AN INSULT) Off to meet Tamara, are we?

MIRANDA: What do you mean, are we? I'm off to meet Tamara for a coffee.

STEVIE: Going for a coffee with Tamara, are we? She's just as much my friend.

MIRANDA: No, she's not because I was the one who made friends with her. You're a friend of a friend. Friendish. Friendoid.

STEVIE: I'm not competing.

MIRANDA: (TEENAGE STYLE) Whatever. You're just jealous because I've found someone else to have fun with.

STEVIE: I have more fun with Tamara. On my fun scale she's eighty-five percent, you're just forty.

MIRANDA: Forty?! Who invented Cake Soup and Roulade Roulette? I'll tell you who. (POINTING AT HERSELF) Captain Fun Times.

STEVIE: Well did I, or did I not, invent Talk as Duncan Bannatyne Day. *OR: Bruce Forsyth, Kirsty Wark, Dick Van Dyke*

MIRANDA: Boring. Very boring game. The game you loved, was my game. Where's Miranda?

EXT. PADDINGTON (FLASHBACK)

Stevie is standing high up somewhere scouring the crowd.

STEVIE: Found her!

Crash-zoom into crowd to pick out Miranda, looking nonchalant. She's wearing red and white striped jumper, bobble hat and round glasses, a la Where's Wally.

Stevie goes up to Miranda. They hug and laugh.

INT. SHOP

Back to present.

Miranda starts to leave.

STEVIE: Opening the door, are we?

MIRANDA: Putting 'are we' after a fact does not make it an insult.

Stevie gets her bag and coat.

What are you doing?

STEVIE: Just taking an early lunch break to meet my friend.

MIRANDA: MY friend.

STEVIE: MY friend.   *Say it quickly jumping in*

Puts on her coat.

MIRANDA: Putting on our coat from Gap Kids, are we?
(TO CAMERA) It does work.

Good enough end to scene? Possibly push each other out of way to get out of door first.

INT. RESTAURANT

Miranda and Stevie walk in trying to get in before each other. They get stuck in the doorway then squeeze in at the same time.

MIRANDA: Clive, Clive – is Tamara here?

CLIVE: She's out buying milk. I'd say she won't be long but she's probably skiving again.

A builder comes out from the kitchen.

BUILDER: (LONDON ACCENT) That's all finished mate, just a loose wing nut to be honest.

MIRANDA / STEVIE: Phwaaaaoooorrr.

Gary looks annoyed/jealous.

BUILDER: Just needed a bit of muscle that's all. You know what I mean?

GARY: Cheers.

Hands over cash. (Doing builder accent and puffing chest up)

GARY: Yeah, thought it was probably the wing nut, somethin' like that. There you go mate, here's the score.

Hands builder cash.

Be lucky.

Builder goes. They stare at Gary.

What?

MIRANDA: (MIMICKING THE ACCENT) You just tried to go all builder alpha male.

GARY: What do you mean tried to? I'm alpha male.

They all shake their heads.

A waiter (Ryan) goes past from kitchen to deliver a meal.

Hang on, just add a bit of parsley.

He puts some parsley delicately on a dish.

MIRANDA/STEVIE/CLIVE: (GIRLISHLY)Just add a bit of parsley.

GARY: (CROSSLY) Alright.

MIRANDA/STEVIE/CLIVE: Oooooh!

Gary looks annoyed, they all turn away from the bar.

GARY: Miranda, can we talk?

They sit at the sofa area.

Listen, have you… thought about us…?

MIRANDA: The us-spending-the-night-together-thingimy? A bit…
(TO CAMERA) I've literally thought of nothing else.

GARY: Great, great because I still really want to give us a chance. I won~~dered if you wanted to go to a hotel or something, if that doesn't sound too sordid.~~ So I wondered if you might want to go on another date this week?

MIRANDA: ~~Sordid away. Sorry.~~

Miranda smiles.

shouldn't
use sordid –
shouldn't seem
sordid. SORDID
is a weird word.
SORDID.

MIRANDA: Yeah, great.

GARY: Great. (SARCASTIC) So I'm alpha male enough for you.

MIRANDA: You! Alpha male! (SHE LAUGHS) Sorry, no sorry.

Tamara comes in. Stevie and Miranda rush towards her.

STEVIE: Tamara!

MIRANDA: Tamara!

STEVIE: Tamara, Tamara…

MIRANDA: (TO THE ANNIE SONG) I love you Tamara…

STEVIE / MIRANDA: (SINGING COMPETITIVELY/HARMONISING)
You're only a day away.

TAMARA: What a lovely welcome. Hey girls.

Puts milk down on the bar and goes to sit down.

CLIVE: I'll put it in the fridge then shall I…? (TUTS) (TO GARY)
I thought you said she was a good waitress in Hong Kong.

GARY: Give it a rest, Clive.

Clive goes to kitchen.

Enough of a seed for audience for later reveal?

TAMARA: So I've just been handed this leaflet – for an art class, painting.
From tonight. I thought maybe it's fate. You up for it?

STEVIE/MIRANDA: Yeah, sure. Yeah, wicked, yeah.

TAMARA: I've always liked art. Do you like Botticelli?

STEVIE/MIRANDA: Oh, amazing. Amazing.

STEVIE: You don't know what Botticelli is.

MIRANDA: Yes I do. It's an ice cream.

Tamara laughs.

Yes obviously that was a joke.

Clocks camera.

STEVIE: So... Boticelli is...?

MIRANDA: Um.

Sees Gary behind Stevie and Tamara mouthing 'a painter'.

A painter.

STEVIE: When did he paint?

MIRANDA: He painted in… um

Sees Gary helping her out by mouthing 'renaissance'.

She tries to understand it.

And starts making noises similar to what he could be making and finally says 'renaissance' but she says it in a weird way having had to find it from Gary.

MIRANDA: He painted in the 'renaissance'. Always said it like that.

STEVIE: And what kind of paintings?

MIRANDA: Big ones, specialising in…

Looks to Gary – the same thing happens. He is mouthing 'nudes'.

Nooo… Nuu… Nuuuud… Nuuuuuudes. He painted Nuuuuuudes in the (HOW SHE SAID IT EARLIER) Renaissance. Yes, count me in.

TAMARA: Great. I'll get some drinks.

Goes.

STEVIE: Nuuuuuuddesss. Being an idiot are we?

Slaps her.

Miranda slaps her back. Two more slaps and then it goes into a silly, girly slap fight. As Tamara approaches Miranda pushes Stevie off her chair.

126

Be good to do it off stool as different – as long as Hadders can do it without crash mat, to keep scene flowing

INT. SHOP (LATER THAT AFTERNOON)

Miranda comes downstairs. Stevie is behind the till.

STEVIE: Coming down the stairs, are we?

MIRANDA: Sitting behind the till, are we?

STEVIE: Using the 'are we', are we?

Penny comes in.

PENNY: Hi darling... Hi Stevie, how are you?

STEVIE: Oh I'm alright but...

PENNY: Oh good. Now look what your hip mother has got herself. (HOLDS UP A MOBILE) A portable phone.

MIRANDA: A mobile. Only twenty years behind.

PENNY: I wasn't going to get one on principle but your father insisted. He said saucy text messages were all the rage. I thought being rude on the phone meant working for BT. (LAUGHS) Now listen, Phylida's cousin, Julian Langtuttington, single, is arranging a vegan barbecue. I mean what is the point. What are they going to do, grill a bread roll? But then again Julian is a little bit (MOUTHED) stupid. He thought pot pourri was a tropical disease. I think he needs (MOUTHED) full-time care.

MIRANDA: Now all I'm seeing is (DEMO).

PENNY: (SHOUTS) full-time care.

MIRANDA: Alright.

PENNY: Phylida's going to text me the details…

MIRANDA: You should've asked, I could have been busy.

Penny and Stevie laugh together, a bit too long. Miranda clocks camera.

PENNY: (GETS A TEXT) A text! Oh bear with, bear with. Such fun.

Penny looks at her phone, putting it close, then far away.

MIRANDA: Oh just wear your glasses…

Penny holds the phone far away from her, straining.

STEVIE: Yeah it's bad for your eyes to strain. I think glasses look very elegant on an older woman.

PENNY: Older woman?

STEVIE: Well you know, a mature lady. A woman of your age.

PENNY: And what age would that be?

STEVIE: Oh ummm…

MIRANDA: Scared.

STEVIE: Six…

Miranda cringes. Penny scorns at everything Stevie says.

Fifty… fifty ni… eigh… fifty six… fou… four… forty-nine. Very elegant. As long as you don't wear them on a chain because that can make you look very old.

PENNY: What do you mean by very old?

MIRANDA: She keeps walking into it.

STEVIE: Old, you know when you're like sixty...

Miranda cringes. Penny looks horrified.

Seve... over a hundred... like your hundred-and-twenties.

PENNY: (TURNING AWAY FROM STEVIE DISGUSTED).
Right, so darling – (AT PHONE) tonight, at...

MIRANDA: Oh, I can't tonight, got plans.

PENNY: (SHOCKED) What?

MIRANDA: An art class. I do things!

PENNY: Miranda, the last time you went out after nine o'clock was when you forgot to put the bins out.

Penny and Stevie laugh.

Miranda clocks camera.

MIRANDA: Excuse me, I have a life.

Penny and Stevie continue to laugh. Miranda goes upstairs. Does a big massive fake laugh and sweeps up.

STEVIE: You do know staying in with fruit friends doesn't count.

MIRANDA: I do not do that…

Looks to camera.

INT. MIRNADA'S FLAT

Miranda is singing Take That 'Shame' to fruit which have faces drawn on them and miniature instruments.

MIRANDA: (SINGING) What a shame we never listened. I told you through the television.
And all that went away was the price we paid.

Speak to Gordon Grapefruit if funny & not too mad?

130

INT. ART CLASS

Tamara, Miranda, Stevie in a row with easels. Few others also in the class.

We reveal Stevie in full beret and painter's outfit. She looks smug.
Miranda raises her eyes.

Helena, the art teacher, comes in. When she speaks, she over emphasises loudly the last word or two of the sentence.

MIRANDA: This is exciting.

TAMARA: Yeah, should be cool.

MIRANDA: Good suggestion. Hey, (SINGING) Once I had a love and it was a gas, soon turned out it was an (SPOKEN) art of class.

Tamara looks blank.

Turns to other art class member:

Hey (SINGS) Once I had a love and it was a gas, soon turned out it was an (SPOKEN) art of class.

They look blank.

Miranda turns to camera.

(SINGS) Once I had a love and it was a gas, soon turned out it was (SPOKEN) an art of class. Oh – whatever…

HELENA: Hello, everybody, welcome to the class. We're together for (LOUDLY) six sessions.

Miranda looks startled.

Twice weekly for (LOUDLY) three weeks. Focusing on (LOUDLY) still life.

Can't use 'Heart of Glass' song to mimic – Gutted!

SONG RIGHTS ARE ANNOYING

131

MIRANDA: Hope it's not food because I'll just want to (LOUDLY) eat it.

Miranda and Tamara laugh.

STEVIE: Stop it.

MIRANDA: I'm just sharing a joke with my friend Tamara.

HELENA: Tonight we start with (LOUDLY) life drawing.

A naked man appears and lies on the chaise longue.

HELENA: So this is Johnny, our life model for tonight.

MIRANDA: And don't forget little Johnny – inappropriate.

Too childish?

They all start painting.

HELENA: (WALKING AROUND) So tomorrow night we'll be doing the female form. Unfortunately our regular model is (LOUDLY) unwell.

Says that by Miranda, who jumps.

HELENA: So if anyone wants to volunteer please do give me a call in the morning...

TAMARA: I life modelled once – so freeing.

MIRANDA: Tamara, that's really brave.

STEVIE: It's good to cross personal boundaries.

MIRANDA: Excuse me, this is a personal conversation.

Stevie slowly paints a long line down Miranda's arm.

STEVIE: Miranda very much stays in her comfort zone.

MIRANDA: That's absolutely not the case. Only last week I had savoury, moved to sweet, then switched back to savoury.

STEVIE: With your nudity issues, seeing a naked man is out of your comfort zone.

MIRANDA: I'm fine with nudity.

Suddenly, looking at the model.

He moved, it moved.

Class stare. Turning round.

Who said that? That is so childish.

STEVIE: Pathetic…

Stevie looks smug.

Miranda paints a line down her face.

We see Stevie is about to retaliate.

Fade to black.

INT. ART CLASS

We see Miranda finish something up on Stevie's face. And then reveal that she has painted Stevie as a tiger.

or cat. Full face paint or mask?

We then reveal Miranda's face has been painted with glasses, beard and moustache.

TAMARA: Hey crazy ladies (RE THEIR FACES), listen, shall we go out?

STEVIE: Yeah when?

TAMARA: Tonight.

MIRANDA: But we *are* out.

TAMARA: Let's go *out* out. To a club…

MIRANDA: Now?!

Looks at her watch.

But it's nearly nine. Four words – Rush. Home. For. *Poirot.*

STEVIE: I'm up for going out out. Miranda's always very in in.

TAMARA: Great, so shall I meet you at the restaurant at eleven?

MIRANDA: Eleven?! I'm up for it. Absolutely. Yeah see you there duuuuuuuudes.

Turns and falls in to an easel – a big crash.

Need this?

INT. RESTAURANT

The restaurant is quiet/winding down for the night.

Miranda walks in, changed for the night and hangs coat up.

MIRANDA: Gary listen I need your help. I've got to stay awake…

Sees Gary chopping a carrot, quickly, with big knife.

GARY: Who said chefs can't be manly.

MIRANDA: You're so sweet.

GARY: Please don't call me sweet.

MIRANDA: Sorry. I need coffee, and something sugary. I'm going out out with Tamara.

He gets coffee and some pavlova.

GARY: You seem obsessed with Tamara at the moment. Pavlova OK?

Starts cutting it.

MIRANDA: There's no need to cut that.

Takes whole plate.

I'm not obsessed with her. She's keeping me young. Plus Stevie thinks she's a better friend.

GARY: Oh no, not one of your stupid competitions again.

INT. SHOP OR FLAT (FLASHBACK)

Miranda and Stevie are standing by an enormous roll of bubble wrap each (size of yoga balls).

GARY: **~~STEVIE~~:** OK first one to pop all their bubbles.

GARY: OK. (WITH STOP WATCH). On your marks, get set. Ready… go!

They unroll the bubble wrap, and start popping by any means possible, rolling up in it, jumping up and down. Doing one big roll along it etc.

INT. RESTAURANT

Back to present.

MIRANDA: Do you ever feel old at thirty-five? It's quite a weird in-between age if you're single isn't it coz most people are at baby stage…

GARY: Are you still single?
I hoped you were off the market.

MIRANDA: Yeah?

GARY: Yeah, because well, I was going to book a room at that new spa hotel for us… if that's OK?

MIRANDA: It is.

He leans over the bar and gives her a kiss on the cheek.

GARY: Great I'll go give them a call.

Goes.

MIRANDA: (TO CAMERA) I could do a little weep of joy.

Stevie comes in, changed for the night.

STEVIE: Drooling over Gary, are we?

MIRANDA: Mutton dressed as lamb, are we?

Tamara comes in. Also changed.

TAMARA: Are you ready to party?

MIRANDA: Yeah, let's go. I'm getting a bit of a high.

TAMARA: Cool, what have you taken?

MIRANDA: Pavlova.

Maybe as they leave M & Stevie do the push to get out of door first competition again.

INT. MIRANDA'S SITTING ROOM. NIGHT

Miranda, Stevie and Tamara pile back in laughing. Tamara singing/dancing.

TAMARA: I can't believe the club closed at two-thirty. More music!

Choose a song. Lady Gaga?

Goes to iPod.

MIRANDA: (GETTING CLOSER TO CAMERA)
Help me, I'm so tired.

The beginning of 'Signed, Sealed, Delivered' comes on — which makes Miranda jump. She starts moving with Tamara.

TAMARA: Where do you go if you want to party till dawn? Come on let's see the sun rise.

Miranda and Stevie look shocked.

This town is so lame. But it must be cool here when you're middle-aged.

STEVIE / MIRANDA: When you're what now please?

TAMARA: Aren't you mid-forties? It doesn't matter does it?

MIRANDA: It does a bit.

Stevie grabs Miranda and heads to the kitchen area.

STEVIE: Middle-aged?!

MIRANDA: Mid-forties?!

STEVIE: Right we'll show her.

Points to objects on counter.

Oh… Hide your *Midsomer Murders* DVDs.

More old age things:- Werthers, Slippers, Knitting ….

MIRANDA: Quick!

Pushes them off counter.

STEVIE: We're not sleeping 'til she sleeps. Deal?

MIRANDA/STEVIE: Foe no more, friend for sure.

Insert the M & Stevie handshake thing & 'LOVE YOU'

TAMARA: (DANCING) This is one of Gary's favourite songs…

STEVIE: (TO MIRANDA) Right, come on, funk down. Show her our stuff.

Starts dancing ott.

Cut to Miranda and Stevie in the kitchen.

Scottish dancing maybe - always feels funny out of context!

MIRANDA: Time?

STEVIE: Three-fifteen

They both do three shots in a row.

MIRANDA: Cola.

STEVIE: Energy drink.

MIRANDA: Coffee.

TAMARA: Come on girls — make-over.

STEVIE: Go on without me, save yourself.

MIRANDA: You can do this.

Miranda slaps Stevie.

Cut to Miranda and Stevie painting their nails. As Miranda leans forward to paint her toes she drops off.

Stevie clashes some cymbals and Miranda sits up.

Lets brave doing the Morecambe & Wise slap. Homage not copying FINE. Surely?

Cut to Miranda and Stevie putting ice cubes down their tops.

Cut to Tamara who is setting up a game.

TAMARA: Love this game!

Miranda and Stevie give themselves electric shocks by licking 9-volt batteries to wake up.

Tamara is watching a DVD. Miranda and Stevie are eating coffee granules.

MIRANDA: More coffee! Come on.

STEVIE: Yes, yes, yes, coffee.

Cut to Miranda and Stevie with two alarm clocks strapped to their ears that are going off. They take them off as Tamara comes over.

TAMARA: It's nine a.m. – too late for sleep. Let's go swimming.

Miranda and Stevie laugh hysterically.

MIRANDA: Oh dear God.

(OOV) Come on.

INT. MIRANDA'S SITTING ROOM

Tamara is by the door. Miranda and Stevie are walking very carefully down the stairs. Miranda stumbles at the last step.

MIRANDA: I thought there was another step but they'd finished. I hate that. (DEMOS)

TAMARA: I'll just get my costume and meet you back here. I find a swim is often better than a sleep. Don't you?

Goes.

MIRANDA: Yes. (TO CAMERA) No. (BEAT) How could swimming be better than a sleep?

TAMARA: (POPS BACK IN). Hey, and let's go shopping later.

Goes.

Miranda and Stevie try to stay upright. They're so tired they seem drunk.

MIRANDA: Shopping?!

Stevie falls to the floor.

MIRANDA: Get up!

Stevie stands up.

MIRANDA: We can do this.

STEVIE: I will not be defeated. We are young. Are you still with me?

They high five but miss.

MIRANDA: I'm still with you.

Gary comes in.

GARY: All right ladies. So Miranda, you wanted to go to a hotel… I've booked a room.

Puts her in a manly hold.

(AS BUILDER) So why don't you come to my bar later and I'll take you there in my transit. Alpha male enough for you?

MIRANDA: Yes.

Gary claps excitedly.

GARY: Yay

MIRANDA: Ruining it.

GARY: Sorry.

GARY: (TO STEVIE) See you later sweet cheeks.

Winks. Goes.

Miranda turns to Stevie who is looking amazed.

STEVIE: Somebody's just been woo-ed.

MIRANDA: That was one hell of a woo.

STEVIE: A hundred woo points to him.

MIRANDA: Welcome to woo central.

STEVIE: It's woo-nderful.

MIRANDA: You ruined it. Stevie, it's actually happening with him. (TO CAMERA) I feel teary again.

Woo-ined. Surely!

TAMARA: (POPS HER HEAD IN) Are you ready? I'll go get changed then but I'll meet you at the swimming pool.

Goes.

MIRANDA: Swimming! I can't … I'll be too tired for tonight…

STEVIE: Now come on.

Runs over to Miranda.

You can do this, or do you want everyone to think you're so old before your time you joined the National Trust just for the gift shops? You'll turn into an even posher version of your, what I call, mother and whenever you taste a cake you'll say…

INT. NATIONAL TRUST CAFE (FLASHBACK)

Miranda in tweeds with a cake.

MIRANDA: (REALLY POSH) Ooh, good lord that's moist. (WAVING) Yoo hoo Marjorie. Have you seen these? (PUTS HER FEET ON THE TABLE TO REVEAL RIDICULOUSLY PATTERNED/COLOURED WELLIES) I don't think they could be more fun. (SEES A GUARDIAN ON THE TABLE) Urh, is that a Guardian? (FLICKS IT AWAY DISGUSTED)

Too much.
End on moist.

INT. SHOP

Back to present.

Miranda leans forward speaking to a stuffed kangaroo.

MIRANDA: That's an excellent point Stevie.

Miranda screams and looks to Stevie.

That's an excellent point. Right.

STEVIE: Right, this is the plan. You go swimming. Then I'll take over and go shopping. She won't know we're sleeping between shifts.

MIRANDA: Brilliant. Between us, we'll make an excellent twenty-something. The stop of us will be untwoable. No. Many lights make hands work. Yes.

They go to high five but lean onto each other asleep.

Come on, right. Swimming things…

Miranda goes to get her swimming things from the kitchen area, falling over onto a beanbag as she goes.

STEVIE: You can do this.

Runs over and crouches by Miranda's face. Picks up Heather Small.

(SINGS) You've got to search inside yourself. (INTO A MEAGAPHONE) (SHOUTS) Get up!

MIRANDA: (SCREAMS, GETS UP) What am I doing here?

STEVIE: Swimming things.

MIRANDA: Swimming things!

Rushes into room. (OOV)

What am I doing in here? (REMEMBERS) Swimming things!

End with Stevie talking to 'Miranda' – but it's a stuffed animal. Giraffe?

INT. SWIMMING POOL

Miranda and Tamara in the changing room. There's another women there. One getting ready to go in, Tamara takes all her clothes off and is already in her bikini.

MIRANDA: Should have changed at home… Fine with it…

Tamara is putting her things in the locker etc.

TAMARA: I'll see you in there.

MIRANDA: Great, yeah, can't wait. Won't be long.

She gets her towel and puts it around her waist and removes her trousers. Then her pants. And keeps the towel tightly around her waist.

Miranda then takes off her top and moves the towel slowly upwards to cover her bra.

We see a woman who has finished swimming come in and take off her swimming costume and stand totally naked to towel herself.

Why, why?

Then she starts putting on her swimming costume — it's quite hard without letting the towel drop. Squats down on the floor to get her costume on her bottom half and falls asleep.

Dreading filming this!

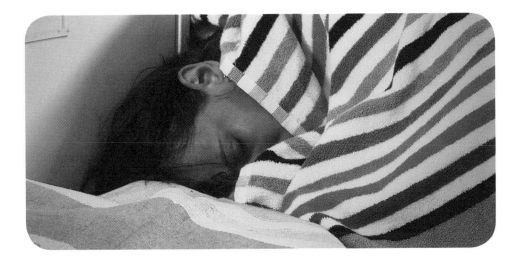

Suddenly the naked woman comes over to where Miranda is to get to her locker. Miranda looks panicked.

MIRANDA: (TO CAMERA) Tit in eye.

Stands up successfully.

Dignity intact.

INT. SHOP

Stevie at the till. Miranda enters.

MIRANDA: I have a massive problem with nudity.

STEVIE: (SARCASTIC) No! Did you keep up with her?

MIRANDA: Yes.

Stevie is pouring a teapot on to a cup held upside down with the tea splashing everywhere.

Are you OK?

STEVIE: Fine.

MIRANDA: Right, OK, focus, I need your help. Because art class, changing room, I'm all cringed out. If I'm going to be woo-ed tonight, Stevie, I've got to find a way to claim nakedity.

STEVIE: OK calm. You just need to normalise it. OK, so the next person who walks through that door just – imagine they're naked.

Penny walks in. Miranda screams.

PENNY: Charming. Darling Phylida has changed the barbecue to tonight so you can come…

MIRANDA: I can't do tonight either.

PENNY: (GETS A TEXT) Ooh a text! Bear with, bear with.

Tries to read it and can't.

Can you read that for me?

MIRANDA: It's Dad. Heading home. Terrible golf game. Come and join me in the bath for a hole in one. I want to show you my loofah. Urh… You've got to wear your glasses!

PENNY: (GIGGLES) I've got a bath to go to.

Penny goes.

MIRANDA: I'm officially cringed out. It's like I've eaten cotton wool. (DEMOS) This can't go wrong with Gary tonight, Stevie, because this is it with him, this is our moment. The night when dos become uno. (PAUSE) Ooh I've had an idea. Oh, it's quite out there: yes, I'm going to ring and say I want to be the life model for the art class. Well if I can get naked with a bunch-o-strangers, there'll be no shyness tonight. I will have claimed my nude-nisity.

Emphasise as from series 1

STEVIE: Go for it. You know you've got to love your body. I do. Well mine – not yours. If I had to rate myself: Hips – ten. Thighs – ten. Breasts – ten.

MIRANDA: (TO CAMERA) Sounds like one of my KFC orders. (LAUGHS)

INT. ART CLASS

Miranda is in a dressing gown in front of the class. Tamara is there.

HELENA: Good evening everybody. This is Miranda, our model for (LOUDLY) tonight.

Miranda jumps.

(TO MIRANDA) We're very excited, very very Rubenesque. (TO CLASS) So you'll see we have curves, contours, undulations…

MIRANDA: Undulations. I'm a woman, not a B road.

HELENA: And because of her height she has an excellent sweep.

MIRANDA: Ooh thank you very much. Keep your eye out for Sooty. (TO CAMERA) Sounded wrong.

Be interesting to see if audience laughs or too naughty/ childish. If they laugh keep.

HELENA: If you want to disrobe and make yourself comfortable.

MIRANDA: Right. Um, OK. No, I can do this. Right. (TO CAMERA) Excuse me.

Pushes the camera down.

(BEAT)
(OOV) I did it!

do it out of vision or a close up of my face?

Tamara does a thumbs up.

TAMARA: Well done!

A beat. The class all replace the canvas on their easels with a larger one.

MIRANDA: (OOV) Rude.

Cut to:

INT. RESTAURANT

Miranda comes into the restaurant — now fully clothed!
(Nice clothes — she looks good)

The restaurant is pretty empty as it's late. The radio is on.

Miranda sees Gary clearing a table, she taps him on the shoulder,
he turns around.

MIRANDA: So are you gonna take this Rubenesque beauty out tonight or what? I've never been more ready.

GARY: Wow. Well yes I am.

Need to perform like M feels really sexy for once.

The radio starts to play 'Let's Get It On'.

They hear it. They are standing by a table, Miranda sweeps everything off it and pulls Gary down on to it.

Miranda suddenly sees a man there halfway through a mouthful and screams.

Music out.

MIRANDA: So sorry sir, do carry on.

MIRANDA / GARY: Sorry.

GARY: Wow, you are… just give me a minute, I'll go get my things.

Runs to the kitchen.

Clive? I'm knocking off early.

Stevie comes in.

Tamara comes in from the kitchen.

STEVIE: Oh here you are. How was it?

TAMARA: She was ace. I think it's one of my best paintings.

MIRANDA: Well when you've got an excellent nuuuuuuude.

Clive comes in.

CLIVE: Tamara, I asked you to clear that table.

TAMARA: Oh yeah, sorry Clive. One sec.

Clive leaves.

So this band is doing a twenty-four-hour gig, dawn till dawn. Wanna come?

MIRANDA: Dawn? (TO STEVIE) I can't go on. (TO TAMARA)
My name's Miranda and my idea of a big night is getting through a giant
Toblerone with an omnibus of *Countryfile*.

STEVIE: Aww.

MIRANDA: Yeah I know, it's lovely. And the only reason I'd be up at dawn
is if I woke up needing the loo.

STEVIE: And my name's Stevie and it's my ambition to grow vegetables
and make my own ratatouille.

MIRANDA: Aw that's lovely.

STEVIE: I know.

MIRANDA: Yeah, kitchen garden.

STEVIE: (TO TAMARA) We're very old…

TAMARA: What's ratatouille?

STEVIE: You don't need to know yet – all in good time.

STEVIE: Just consider us, your Auntie Miranda and Auntie Stevie…

Miranda sees Gary beckoning her. Miranda slips away and creeps out of the restaurant with Gary.

Clive comes in.

CLIVE: Are you still gossiping? Right, that's it, you're fired.

TAMARA: Clive, sorry.

She goes to kitchen.

CLIVE: Sorry Gary, but you only employed her because she's your wife or whatever the set up is…

Miranda and Gary stop dead. Gary is saying 'no no' to Clive.

I didn't say anything…

MIRANDA: No you did, you said she's your wife.

STEVIE: Who's his wife?

MIRANDA: Is Tamara your wife?

GARY: No, not really. (NERVOUSLY) Technically she's my wife…

MIRANDA: (STUNNED) What?

GARY: Doesn't matter. I'll explain on the way to the hotel… come on…

CLIVE: (SO EXCITED) Oh my — are you two together…?

MIRANDA: Sorry, Tamara's your wife.

CLIVE: Were you two eloping?

MIRANDA: Clive shush…

Tamara comes out of the kitchen.

TAMARA: Clive…

STEVIE: Married to Gary, are we?

GARY: Miranda, I can explain…

MIRANDA: No no, Gary. I don't know what to say…

We hear Ronan Keating's 'You Say It Best When You Say Nothing At All'

Clive! Can you switch that off please?

We reveal Clive at the CD player.

CLIVE: Sorry.

He switches it off.

MIRANDA: I was trying to do an angry rant to storm out to… I did a life class for you…

She tires and can't think of anything.

Oh forget it.

Goes.

GARY: Miranda…

Goes after her.

INT. MIRANDA'S SITTING ROOM/CORRIDOR

Miranda storms in. Gary runs in after her. Tension is very high.

MIRANDA: Sorry, what do you mean you're married?

GARY: OK, she's a friend from Hong Kong and for a pass to study here I said I'd do the green card thing for a visa. I know I'm an idiot. But I owed her a massive favour. Come on, it's not like I'm still sleeping with her…

Realises what he just said.

MIRANDA: Still? Gary, still?

Not too mean of Gary hopefully. Tom will deliver with bit of charm on it.

GARY: Sorry, sorry… it was a while ago; it was when I was travelling. It was just a fling.

MIRANDA: And you let me become friends with her. You knew what a big thing this was for me, Gary. But it was obviously not real for you because if you really cared you wouldn't keep such a massive secret. Taking me to a hotel room wasn't another romantic gesture – it was another meaningless fling, only this one won't end in marriage.
(TO CAMERA) Now, that was quite good.

She storms out.

In the corridor.

(OOV) But I've stormed out of my own flat.

Knocks on the door. He opens it.

You get out…

GARY: Let's talk about it please. I only didn't tell you because I knew you'd overreact.

MIRANDA: (FURIOUS) Overreact?!

GARY: (EQUALLY FURIOUS) It doesn't mean anything. It was a favour for a friend. So you've done everything perfectly in your life have you?

MIRANDA: That's not the point. I can't talk about this now.

Tries to slam the door but Gary is in the way.

Can you please get out of the way so I can slam the door.

He steps inside. She slams the door.

You're meant to be on the other side. We can't even do arguing properly.

He starts to go. Miranda slams the door. But it catches him.

GARY: Ow!

MIRANDA: A real man wouldn't have felt that.

Slams door.

Flops on the sofa. Close to tears.

I'm so tired but I'm too angry and upset to go to sleep…

Falls asleep.

INT. RESTAURANT (MORNING)

Miranda comes in.

Clive plays 'Didn't We Almost Have It All'.

MIRANDA: How long have you been hovering over that play button?

CLIVE: Forty minutes.

GARY: Morning.

MIRANDA: Morning.

A customer comes up to the bar to look at the menu.

(TO CUSTOMER) Oh yes they do a lovely breakfast here. Comes with egg, two sausages, and a green card.

They sit at the sofas where they sat at the top of the show.

GARY: Please tell me we can move on from this?

MIRANDA: Yes, I do want to move on from this...

GARY: Really? Thank you, thank you. Listen. Tamara's gone. She thought it was best to get out of the way. I only didn't tell you because...

MIRANDA: No, Gary wait... I'm moving on from you, us...
I never know what you want – and when I finally thought that you knew,
there was some massive lie.
(CLOSE TO TEARS) And I can't handle it. You know so... you'll never get to
see my naked sweep.

Gary sighs, upset/angry, gets up.

Sorry.

GARY: (ANNOYED) What is this? (RE SOMETHING BEHIND THE
BAR THAT IS IN HIS WAY)

CLIVE: Tamara left it for the restaurant. An apology gift.

*Hands Gary a big canvas. He puts it standing against a chair and stares at it.
We don't see the picture.*

GARY: Wow. So that's your naked sweep...

Miranda sees it.

MIRANDA: Ah. No. Gary don't look. Don't. No.

Stevie and Penny walk in.

What's everyone doing here? Nobody look.

Miranda dives under a table.

(TO CAMERA) Well this is a new low.

The Tony Hart Gallery music starts.

You have been watching comes up on the screen:

Miranda Hart under the table.

We pan along the others, all staring at the picture.

They don't wave, or look to camera, we just see their reactions to the painting.

Tom Ellis: looking appreciatively.

Patricia Hodge: squinting, she puts her glasses on and screams.

Sarah Hadland: looking through her fingers

James Holmes: in hysterics

BUILDER: Nice undulations.

A You Have Been Watching to reflect down mood of episode

Miranda looks shocked to camera.

Series Two, Episode Four:
Behind the Scenes Tit-Bits

Paul Kerensa, one of the writers who helps with gags at the end of the writing process, came up with the cut away of Miranda and Stevie playing 'Where's Miranda?' He and I had no idea that it would end up with teenagers playing their own version of Where's X? in shopping centres in various British cities. I love that! And I am very grateful to Paul for that gag. Over the three series I had to come up with way too many flashbacks of games and competitions for Miranda and Stevie.

Anna Chancellor is one of my favourite actresses and getting her to play the art teacher was a massive boost for us all.

We had a debate whether we should see the nude picture of me at the end of the episode or not. I am very glad we didn't for mine and the nation's sake.

My favourite line to say in this episode: 'But it's nearly nine. Four words: Rush. Home. For. Poirot.' I get it quoted at me a lot, which reassures me I am not the only one who likes to be sofa- or bed-bound by 9 p.m.

For me, the Gary character comes alive for the first time in this episode. He is no longer just a foil for Miranda and no longer just a super nice guy. Tom always made him more dimensional than he was on the page. But I finally nailed Gary in the writing in this episode.

Just Act Normal

. . .

As I said, the sitcom is very much episodic, apart from the will-they-won't-they through line, so each show feels like a very different beast and that makes it hard to have favourites. However, if you put a gun to my head (and please don't) and asked me which I would plump for (good word, plump) I would have to say, this is my favourite.

Because I had lumped (good word, lump) so much in to the other episodes of Series Two there was a 'missing sixth episode'. The Gary and Miranda story worked over five episodes not six and there weren't many Post-It note ideas left on the office wall. I had the idea of Miranda and Penny in a therapist's office. But just as a scene. Then writer Richard Hurst persuaded me that it could sustain a whole 'bottle' episode. Sitcoms set in one room are known as bottle episodes. I was hesitant but then we began to talk about what could happen, how the mother and daughter relationship could be explored comedically and I got a little excited. It also meant less story. Hurrah. Fewer graphs, less of a house of cards. We still had to make sure things happened and there was some kind of story and tension there, but it was one linear plot. I then had the freedom to write considerably more dialogue and jokes for the characters rather than being held prisoner by a complex set of scenes all serving a particular purpose, as in other episodes. Stop press: don't choke on your donut or whatever snack of choice you are indulging in, but I think I may have actually enjoyed writing this episode.

The director, Juliet May, got very excited about it when she read it. She thought it really could work. But as we went in to rehearsals we all became a little jittery. We were basically doing a one-act play on television. And never more has the studio audience sitcom been presented so crudely as the tricky beast it is than for this episode. This leads me nicely, almost as if I had planned it, in to telling you: How a Studio Audience Sitcom is Made.

We recorded in front of the audience on Sunday nights. We do a five day week so this meant meeting on Wednesday morning at 9 a.m. sharp to do the read-through. Actors and crew have all had the scripts before the read-through, but only four days before we are recording are we sitting down to read it through together for the first time. There will then be a script meeting with the script editor, producer and director. We will iron out any story issues, listen to any producer concerns, and cut out some of the stuff that we didn't have time for. It's always easier to wait to hear the actors read it before you decide which is the weaker dialogue and which jokes to delete. After giving the actors the changes, we start rehearsing. This will be at about 11.30 a.m. on Wednesday. At this point I have to take a deep breath and not start fretting and clock-watching. But you can't help but be aware that we have three days to rehearse a half-hour piece of television. It's not a one-off live play in front of 350 people. It's a one-off live play in front of 350 people that will be recorded for television, that will then be your legacy on screen forever more. Very deep breath and we start at the beginning and block through the episode on day one.

We call it Funny Wednesday. Everyone is enjoying the lines, embellishing, making suggestions, we get the giggles, we are deeply concentrated on the director's blocking, it's a fun day. Then Thursday comes. We have all had a night on our own to go over our lines and question our abilities as performers, we have all done the scenes twice over already, it doesn't feel funny any more. And then we all remind each other – this happens every Thursday. It's unfunny Thursday. It just *feels* unfunny. Just go through the motions, learn, keep blocking it and try not to worry. The next morning you wake up to Funny Friday. The adrenalin is running now, you are off script, you have to find the funny again. This is our last day to rehearse and the executives and all the crew are coming in to watch at 2 p.m. It's a frantic morning. The crew rehearsal is always agony. We run it from beginning to end in the rehearsal room with the mocked out sets and limited props and furniture. And we all tend to feel like children doing a terrible play to our parents. The crew are focusing on their scripts and what their job will be on the night of the record. People aren't really watching it as a show so there isn't always laughter because of that. But EVERY Friday we huddle in a paranoia of actors – which I think should be the collective noun for actors, or the me me me of actors – afterwards all thinking 'But my bit didn't get a laugh', 'We are going to die in front of that audience', 'I cocked that line up again, I am never going to get it right on the night'. Pathetic beasts, we are. We get our notes from the execs, make a few changes and that's it. We may do a few line runs on the Saturday. But Saturday we are in the studio pre-recording some things we can't do in front of the audience. For example, things that might involve animals (the goat). Or things that are very messy like Miranda and Stevie eating jelly with boxing gloves. Or things that are massive costume changes that we won't have time to do on the night. Like Stevie falling in to a bubble bath.

And then it's Sunday. And for the first time we are rehearsing with the cameras. We start at 9 a.m. and the audience comes in at 7 p.m. Again you are hit in the face by the frankly insane pressure there is to make television this way. We have just the day to rehearse it on the right set, getting our moves perfect so the cameras catch us correctly, finalise plotting the camera script – which camera shoots who and what angle, make sure the jokes work on camera, a dress rehearsal at 4 p.m., a brief 45 minute break at 6 p.m. then make up checks and we are in front of the audience, doing three takes maximum per scene. Usually only two. A half-hour sitcom takes about three hours to record. It's fast paced. And a bit like running a marathon to perform solidly for three hours.

But when you hear the first laugh you remember this is the ultimate. Theatre on television. And my style of comedy, for this sitcom at least, needs an audience. You need to punctuate the lines with a laugh, the rhythm of the dialogue needs to be performed to an audience otherwise it doesn't have the same energy and resonance of delivery. We hear a laugh and everything from the week is forgiven. We're off.

INT. THERAPIST'S OFFICE

The (private) therapist's room is very big and quite smart. It has a desk with big, high backed wheely chair – which you can lean back in.

There is a sofa facing the desk with little tables on either side. There are an unnecessary amount of other occasional tables and chairs (another desk chair that has adjustable settings, rocking chair).

There are bookshelves and a table behind the sofa stacked with magazines, and tea/coffee making facitilies.

There is a water cooler and a filing cabinet and a few things that make it look officey, but essentially it has a smart drawing-room effect with lots of pictures and ornaments.

Miranda is sitting in a rocking chair. She is looking smarter than normal.

MIRANDA: (TO CAMERA) Well hello to you. Now, for the eagle-eyed amongst you, you'll see I'm not at home. I'm actually at a psychiatrist's office. For those who said 'about time', rude. No I'm not here for a session as such but um… well I can't explain now – sorry I'm feeling a bit anxious. I'm not sure I should have chosen the rocking chair. It's meant to be re-laxing but um… if you get the speed wrong you look a bit manic. (DEMOS) Right, let's all just calm down shall we and crack on with the show…

OPENING TITLES

INT. THERAPIST'S OFFICE

Miranda is pacing nervously. Penny comes in.

PENNY: That was a lovely loo. I do like a nice loo. Lovely soap. Smell my hands.

MIRANDA: I don't want to smell your hands.

PENNY: Smell them!

Penny puts them by Miranda's nose who bats them away.

MIRANDA: Get off!

PENNY: (PEERING OUT OF DOOR) He was still on the phone. Should be here in a mo.

Miranda goes to get some water from the water cooler.

MIRANDA: Sounds like a fart in a bath. (LAUGHS)

Penny looks disapproving. Miranda stops laughing.

Miranda then realises the water tap is stuck and water keeps pouring out.

Oh, oh help! The tap's stuck, quick!

PENNY: Oh for goodness' sake.

MIRANDA: Get me another cup.

She does.

Get another one…

PENNY: There aren't any more.

Miranda starts filling the cup and drinking.
Penny is trying to stop the tap – general faffing.

MIRANDA: Find a ~~bin~~! receptacle.

Penny grabs a bin and holds it up.

PENNY: Here we are.

MIRANDA: That's wicker. It's wicker.

Water is going everywhere.

Hold this. Drink that.

Penny tries to fiddle with the tap.

I need to find a receptacle. GOOD WORD!

MIRANDA: I've found a receptacle.

Miranda gets his briefcase from the desk and starts filling that up with water.

Penny manages to unplug the tap and the water stops.

MIRANDA: Oh I've got water in his case!

Miranda starts to drink from his briefcase to remove evidence.

Suddenly he (Anthony, the therapist) comes in. Anthony is dapper, high status, aged 40s/50s.

MIRANDA/PENNY: Hello.

*ANTHONY Hopkins.
Only I will know!
FUN*

PENNY: You must be Doctor Hopkins… good afternoon…

Anthony walks to his desk.

Miranda puts his briefcase back.

MIRANDA: Good afternoon, sorry, I was just drinking from your briefcase, which might sound a little odd, it's just I'd wet the floor. You know, I hadn't wee-ed on it.

PENNY: (SOTTO VOCE) Will you shut up.

(TO ANTHONY) Sorry. Now I just want to say, that we're not here for a session. It was all a silly misunderstanding. There was a little, what I call, incident, which the police unnecessarily got involved in. It's a long story, we won't bore you. But to stop Miranda being arrested and charged, I said she was… (MIMES MAD) one pashmina short of a wardrobe.

MIRANDA: I'm not.

PENNY: She's not. But the police insisted we get an assessment from a psychiatrist…

MIRANDA: That's you.

They curtsey.

PENNY: That's you. They initially put me in touch with one on the (MOUTHED) NHS. Well I said, I'm not going (MOUTHED) NHS, thank you very much. I mean, what are we, crack whores?

Miranda looks surprised at her.

So, we just need to sit here for a session, to tell them we've been. Well obviously. I like to think on first meeting one can tell I am of sound mind. I mean I vote Conservative and my tea of choice is Lapsang Souchong, need I say more. (LAUGHS CHARMINGLY) So, can we sit anywhere?

Hearing Patricia say this is making me laugh a lot! Go PH. ♥

MIRANDA: We don't need a session. So, can we sit anywhere?

Anthony just gestures towards the chairs.

MIRANDA: Wait, wait mum. There are so many chairs it might be a psychological test which chair we plump for? Ooh, that's a good word, 'plump'.

Plump.
(TO ANTHONY) Plump.
(TO CAMERA) Plump.

PENNY: Just sit down.

She sits on the sofa.

MIRANDA: You have a lot o'chairs.

Sees a chair.

MIRANDA: Is this one of those ergonomic ones is it?

Sits on it, fiddles with a lever and the chair rises up much higher.

MIRANDA: Up she goes.

Then she pushes the lever and the chair goes down again.

Penny gives her a withering look.

There is a silence.

Anthony looks at them blankly.

And down she blows. (LAUGHS) Oh it's a lovely chair isn't it?

Spins around and waves at Anthony.

Hello.

She pushes herself across the room ending up by a sideboard.

Comes across a plastic pot of flowers.

She pushes a button and the flowers start turning and play music.

MIRANDA: Oh, oh it doesn't stop. It's one of those, you have to wait sorry.

I'll just have to let it go.

Starts dancing a little to it.

PENNY: Oh, (STARTS MOVING) such fun.

Mranda dances a bit more. It suddenly stops.

They could do a similar or same dance move.

MIRANDA: Oh, comes to a very sudden end.
(TO FLOWERS) You made me look like a fool.

Penny beckons Miranda over to the sofa to sit with her.

PENNY: (SOTTO VOICE TO MIRANDA)
For goodness' sake, just act normal.

MIRANDA: It's nigh on impossible to act normal when you're trying to act normal. I'm so self-conscious. I don't know how to sit. Hands on knees (DEMOS). Legs crossed? Legs apart? Sort of feel like I've got too many legs.

Miranda wriggles in chair and ends up in a very awkward position.

PENNY: How is that normal?

MIRANDA: It's too hard. Psychiatrist is staring at us and not talking.

PENNY: (TO ANTHONY) Hello again.

MIRANDA: Hello!

PENNY: Perhaps we should explain why we're here, in case you were thinking us a little, what I call, odd. Simple story.

MIRANDA: You see I was at an ice cream van in a park, and this kid ran over my foot with his wheely trainers and I dropped my ice cream.

PENNY: She overreacted and got cross with this little boy…

MIRANDA: Overreacted? I could see my dollop, another excellent word, dollop… of freshly whipped ninety-nine was in the dirt – that's an upsetting situation for anyone. Overreacted. Has the world gone mad?

Too many "words" cut this, save moist & plinth for later. Think better.

PENNY: She demanded that the little boy get her a new ice cream, and he exploded into tears just as this very charming man was jogging past…

MIRANDA: He wasn't that charming.

PENNY: He was charming enough for you, (AGGRESSIVELY TO MIRANDA) in that he was a man with a pulse. (CHARMINGLY TO ANTHONY) Anyway, the man stopped to see if everything was all right.

MIRANDA: And to explain why I was cross with this little boy I told a little lie and said that I was his teacher.

PENNY: Anyway, suddenly the twenty-nine other children from this boy's class appeared demanding ice creams.

MIRANDA: Which I had to get them because I was 'the teacher'.

PENNY: And then the man jogged on… I said to Miranda, quick jog after him, keep chatting I'll get the ice creams (LAUGHS).

MIRANDA: But I didn't follow him.

PENNY: No she didn't jog after him, then the real teacher appeared wanting to know why I was buying twenty-nine ice creams for children I'd never met. So we ran, well galloped…

Miranda and Penny demo.

MIRANDA: We galloped… cos it's fun isn't it? It's fun to gallop. And the children followed us.

PENNY: The children followed and then the teacher thought Miranda was trying to kidnap them. Unfortunately there was a policeman in the area who became very suspicious.

MIRANDA: Not helped by the fact that the ice cream van was following us because we forgot to pay for the ice creams.

PENNY: Anyway, to cut a long story short, once the armed response team had been stood down, we had to go to the station where I explained that Miranda was one stick short of a lolly… didn't take much convincing.

Pointing at Miranda.

MIRANDA: They thought it was hereditary…

Pointing at Penny.

So they let us off as long as we had an assessment.

PENNY: So you see we just need to sit here for the session. We don't need a, what I call, assessment.

MIRANDA: Well it's also what I call an assessment isn't it.

(TO CAMERA) We all call it an assessment. An assessment is an assessment. (TO ANTHONY) You'd call it an assessment if you spoke.

Miranda gets up and wanders around the office. She comes across a china duck.

MIRANDA: (TO THE DUCK) Hello, how are you? Quack, quack – oh really, you are funny.

She notices the therapist looking at her and clocks camera worried.

(TO CAMERA) Really shouldn't do things like that in front of a psychiatrist.

On a shelf behind Anthony's desk are some Russian dolls.

MIRANDA: Ooh I like these.

She removes each of them.

Hello I'm the mammoth one. Hello I'm the average one. And bonjourno I'm the tiny one.

Miranda bangs the top and bottom half of the Russian doll together. It sounds like horses hooves.

Miranda, whilst Anthony is not looking, gallops behind his desk making the hoof noise.

As he turns she stops and puts them down. Miranda picks up a telescope.

Do you have a naval background? (IN PIRATE VOICE) Ahargh me hearties.

She looks in it.

We suddenly see a massive Penny.

Miranda screams.

Handwritten note: Talking to a duck – too mad!

We see that Penny has approached Miranda.

She grabs the telescope, and walks Miranda back to the sofa.

PENNY: (SOTTO VOCE) You are coming across as nutty. I will not have him thinking that we have got problems. Look at him, poised to write in his pad.

They smile at him.

Just sit quietly. It's not for long. Act normal.

MIRANDA: I was being normal.

PENNY: You were being a horse with a Russian doll.

MIRANDA: I'm thirsty.

Could leave little pauses. Think Noel Coward's Hayfever.

178

Looks at water cooler.

PENNY: Don't. Have some coffee.

Penny reads. Miranda gets a cup of coffee from the table behind the sofa.

She presses down the coffee flask.

MIRANDA: Ooh, it's a very confident jet isn't it? — Sort of a bit like a horse weeing. A horse has a very brazen wee.

Off Penny's look.   **THEY DO!**

> Sorry.
> (TO ANTHONY) Sorry.
> (TO CAMERA) Sorry.

She goes to sit down with her cup.

ANTHONY: So…

Penny and Miranda scream.

Miranda spills coffee on her lap. She leaps up.

MIRANDA: Oooh, hot coffee, hot coffee, hot coffee in sensitive parts. And I hate a wet pant. I'm going to have to take my trousers off…

PENNY: (TO ANTHONY) I'm so sorry…

She gets the throw on the back of the sofa.

MIRANDA: I shall use this as a sarong if I may.

ANTHONY: That's quite an expensive silk-mix throw.

MIRANDA: Well a pair of tough titties to you sir. I'm not wandering around in my pants. And if you say you'd rather that than me wearing your silk-mix throw, then you are dirty.

In a deft move, she puts the throw round her waist and takes her trousers off.

She hangs her trousers up to dry. And comes back, showing off her sarong.

MIRANDA: (SUDDENLY BREAKS INTO HAWAIIAN DANCE)
Hula hula! Hula hula! Hula hula!

Laughs.

Cos of the sarong.

Anthony picks up his pen.

ANTHONY: So Miranda. Question?

MIRANDA: (SINGING) Tell me what you think about me...
Beyonce...

ANTHONY: Question...

WONDER IF UNI MATES WILL REMEMBER WE DID THIS! 92–'95

MIRANDA: Tell me how you think about this... sorry that's quite hard not to do actually.

ANTHONY: Interesting. You seem to be avoiding the question.
So Miranda, do you often lie?

MIRANDA: No.(TO CAMERA) I just did.

PENNY: You are so kind to show an interest, but there's nothing to discuss. We're only here so we can say that we've been. I'll pay of course. In fact, how much do you charge?

Gets out her cheque book.

ANTHONY: It's two hundred pounds.

MIRANDA / PENNY: Two hundred pounds!

Beat

Two hundred pounds!

Beat.

They look at each other.

They look back at him.

Two hundred pounds!

MIRANDA: Should have gone on the (MOUTHED) NHS. For two hundred pounds you should ask him why you mouth (MOUTHED) certain words. Although usually you get them the wrong way round.

PENNY: What do you mean?

MIRANDA: Well the other day at the surgery you said, Wendy has been (MOUTHED) diagnosed (NORMALLY) clinically obese. She heard.

PENNY: Well you mouth words. Say sex.

MIRANDA: (MOUTHED) Sex. Psychiatrist present.

They smile at him.

ANTHONY: So is there anything you'd like to talk about to make use of this time?

MIRANDA: No, no.

PENNY: Oh, no, no. We don't want to start talking about our childhoods. Particularly Miranda's. Such an ugly baby. (LAUGHS) Her father suggested we put the babygrows on upside down. (LAUGHS) Such fun.

ANTHONY: Do you want to talk about that, Miranda?

MIRANDA: No, no, don't want to talk childhood, 'Oh, she got rid of my dog when I was eleven'. Although she did.

PENNY: Well, it kept poo-ing in the house.

MIRANDA: Only because you didn't let her out regularly for, what I call, poo-portunities. I could blame you for...

PENNY: Psychiatrist present.

They smile at him. A beat. Penny looks at her watch.

Penny takes out a tissue.

Miranda starts wriggling on the sofa.

PENNY: What's the problem?

MIRANDA: I've got an awkward itch. I'm going to have to do a fast walk to get rid of it.

She does so in a circle around the room. Then gallops.

That's got it.

Anthony looks up.

Sorry I was just having a little wander around.

Miranda finishes her circular walk.

Beat.

We get people in our shop who do a little circular walk like that –
we like to call it the sweep browse. You know when you come in to a shop
and you immediately think, 'Oh no this isn't what I was expecting, there's
nothing here that I want', but I can't suddenly leave cos that would look
rude. So I have to do this sort of (DEMOS) 'Oh that's nice' and then go.
The sweep browse (DEMOS).

Beat.

Good word, browse. Browse.

Pause.

MIRANDA: Browse. Yeah she's a lovely word. See her as a female word.
Thurst – male word. The queen of all words of course, moist. The king of all
words – plinth. (BEAT) Imagine a moist plinth. Lovely.

PENNY: Do you think you could stop talking at some point?

MIRANDA: Yes. Easy.

She starts humming.

PENNY: No humming.

She stops humming and starts whistling.

No whistling.

Miranda starts to mime singing.

Miranda looks from side to side.

PENNY: No playing eyeball tennis.

M MIMES SINGING
PENNY: No pretending
you're singing at
Wembley

Miranda does an 'ooooh' face to camera.

Penny yawns, Miranda yawns. Beat. Anthony yawns.

MIRANDA: Oh dear, we're in a yawn loop.

Penny starts to yawn.

Don't yawn. Oh no.

Miranda yawns.

Anthony yawns. They all yawn.

PENNY: And now we're all yawning.

Save 'yawn
catching' joke
for something
else

Miranda puts her coffee cup back.

Then Anthony writes in his pad.

Penny stands up shocked. They are panicked.

PENNY: (TO ANTHONY) What are you writing down? And about whom? (TO MIRANDA) Act normal.

He continues to write.

MIRANDA: Stop saying that I'm just standing here.

Anthony stops writing and puts his pad down.

Anthony goes to look at a book and stands by a shelf.

PENNY: (WHISPERING) Who does he think he is? Thinking that we've got problems. He's a (MOUTHED) complete (LOUDLY) bastard

ARSE

MIRANDA: Wrong way round.

PENNY: Go and find out what he's written.

MIRANDA: Good idea. Cover me.

Anthony is still standing with his back to the room reading.

Miranda dives down, rolls on to the floor and pops up by the desk.

Miranda pops her head up above the table to have a look at the pad but Anthony is about to turn back.

PENNY: (SUDDENLY SHOUTS) Me! Me! Look at me! Me.

Anthony turns to her.

(SINGING) Me and my girl... meant for each other...

Miranda creeps back behind Anthony.

(SINGING) Sent for each other, and liking it so...

MIRANDA / PENNY: (SINGING) Me and my girl, no use pretending.
We knew the ending a long time ago.

They bow.

PENNY: Just a bit of Noel Gay...

They sit down.

At uni I must have seen Me & My Girl 100's of time at ♪ Bristol Hippodrome. TRAGIC!

MIRANDA: I couldn't read it. It was in shorthand.

PENNY: (SUDDENLY LOUDLY/CROSS) Well if you'd concentrated more at secretarial college...

MIRANDA: Oh, here we go. (TO ANTHONY) This is the kind of thing...
(CROSS) I didn't want to go to secretarial college.

PENNY: You can't be happy running a joke shop.

MIRANDA: Joke slash gift. And yes I am happy.

PENNY: Thirty-five, running a joke shop...

MIRANDA: Joke slash gift!

PENNY: No wonder you can't get a man.

MIRANDA: I had a man. Nearly. (TO ANTHONY) Gary. But the idiot messed that up. I don't want to talk about him. I've moved on.

ANTHONY: Is that true?

MIRANDA: Absolutely yes. I don't think about him. Don't miss him. No. I mean if you're asking me if I act out imaginary conversations with him using a painted plate on top of a mop, then no.

Clocks camera.

We hear a knocking on the door.

ANTHONY: Come in?

Gary pops his head around.

PENNY: Talk of the devil. What are you doing here?

GARY: Sorry, Stevie told me you were here. Look I know you are in the middle of something but I just couldn't wait to see you, Miranda.

He comes over to Miranda and pulls her up from the sofa.

I can't handle it if you'll never forgive me, I can't get you out of my mind. I'm in love with you.

He gives her an incredibly romantic, gentle kiss with his hands on her face.

We see Miranda smile/nearly weep.

He gets down on one knee as if to propose.

Miranda, will you…?

We then jump cut to Miranda with the same face, sitting where she was before, it was a fantasy.

PENNY: (OOV) Miranda?

MIRANDA: Ummm... yes, no don't think about him. Don't miss him. (TO PENNY) And my shop is enough of a career.
PENNY: Well, if you call wasting your life a career.

MIRANDA: (REALLY ANGRY) What I call a waste of life is you wasting your life worrying about me wasting my life!

ANTHONY: I think we're making progress.

PENNY: We are not making progress! We don't need progress or a session. (ANGRY AT MIRANDA) Act normal!

ANTHONY: Maybe it might help if you saw things from each other's perspective. Perhaps try a bit of role play – Miranda as Penny, Penny as Miranda...

MIRANDA: (STILL FURIOUS) Fine. Good idea. (IMPRESSION) Oh hello everyone...

ANTHONY: Haven't quite explained...

MIRANDA: ...don't I look marvellous...

ANTHONY: Right.

MIRANDA: ...look at me please, I want be the centre of, what I call, attention. Now, gossip for you, Geoffrey Warburton has been (MOUTHED) paying for (NORMALLY) prostitutes. Rah rah rah this is talking without actually saying anything rah ra radiddy rah, snorty laugh, hair flick, hair flick, keeping up appearances rah rah rah (LAUGHS.) Envy me, envy me…

Looks smugly at Penny.

ANTHONY: I didn't just mean insulting each other…
PENNY: (FURIOUS IMPRESSION) Well hello, I'm Miranda…

ANTHONY: Oh dear.

PENNY: I'll just waddle over here.

Starts walking like Miranda.

And waste more of my life.

Looking at a picture of plums.

Ooh, you've got nice plums, as it very much were.

She does a cheeky grin to camera.

(TO CAMERA) Aren't I naughty? —

Miranda looks shocked. Clocks camera herself.

Oh, look there's Gary, (WALKING AGAIN) isn't he delicious, but not as delicious as this pie…

MIRANDA: Excuse me what was that walk?

PENNY: It's a lollop.

MIRANDA: I do not lollop.

PENNY: You lollop. You are one of life's lollopers. You should be a lollopop lady. (LAUGHS)

Handwritten note (pointing to "Aren't I naughty?"): Wonder whether that is breaking the convention too much. Will see what audience reaction is ....

Handwritten note in heart: PLEASE LAUGH BBC AUDIENCE ! Helllpppp

MIRANDA: Wait for it.

PENNY: Such fun.

MIRANDA: There it goes. (IMPERSONATING PENNY) Such fun! Have you met my daughter Miranda? I have no respect for any of her life choices… and at Easter we give her a rice cake hunt instead of a chocolate egg hunt, such fun.

PENNY: (IMPERSONATING MIRANDA) I'm Miranda and although my mother has done everything possible to improve my life I'm incredibly ungrateful. And very clumsy. Oh look, here I go falling over again.

Penny falls over onto the sofa. *Or should we get Penny to do MASSIVE fall?!*

190

ANTHONY: Well that was all very interesting.

PENNY: (TO MIRANDA) This is exactly what wasn't meant to happen. We've just got to sit here for a few more minutes – he'll refer us for more sessions if we're not careful.

PENNY / MIRANDA: Best behaviour.

They smile at Anthony. He smiles back.

A pause.

Miranda sees a bowl of fruit.

MIRANDA: Is that real fruit?

ANTHONY: What do you mean?

MIRANDA: I mean, is that fruit real?
(TO CAMERA) I don't know how to make it clearer.

PENNY: Is this fruit part of the two hundred pounds.

MIRANDA / PENNY: Two hundred pounds?!

ANTHONY: I suppose it is in a sense, yes.

PENNY: Oh well in that case.

She goes to get the fruit bowl and tips the whole lot in her bag.

Excuse me.

Miranda goes to her bag.

She gets out some food – scotch eggs, sandwiches and crisps and lays it on the floor.

Penny is staring at her.

ANTHONY: May I ask what you're doing?

MIRANDA: I'm playing a round of golf. (LAUGHS) (TO CAMERA) It's funny because I'm not. (TO ANTHONY) Having a picnic. Do you mind?

PENNY: What are you doing?

MIRANDA: Washing an elephant. LAUGHS (TO CAMERA) Did it again. (TO PENNY) I'm having a spot o lunch.

PENNY: (CROSS) You see this is the kind of the thing…

MIRANDA: I can explain. I got up a bit late today and for breakfast all there was, was a tea cake, so I had that. And then I was still hungry by late noon, so had a sausage sandwich, which was a kind of breakfast, so now I've got out of sync and owe myself a lunch. (TO ANTHONY) I'd offer you something, but I don't share food as a rule. Freaks me right out.

TRUE as Hadders knows from the Snack a Jacks 'incident' !

PENNY: (CROSS) You see this is the kind of the thing… always been obsessed with food.

MIRANDA: (GETTING CROSS NOW TOO) I'm not obsessed with food.

Reaches into her bag and pulls out an entire roast chicken.

PENNY: And this from the woman who when mistaken for being pregnant,

joined the local mothers-to-be group, because, and I quote, 'They have free tea and biscuits and people randomly feel my breasts, it's the best fun I've ever had'.

MIRANDA: Mum you're making me sound weird.

PENNY: You're the one sitting on a psychiatrist's floor having a picnic lunch at four in the afternoon.

193

MIRANDA: Fine. I shall eat it later.

Miranda packs everything back into her bag.

I'll just…

Miranda tears a leg off the chicken before putting it away.

Anthony offers her a box of tissues to wipe her greasy hands.

MIRANDA: Actually that would be very… Can be a bit sticky can't they?

Miranda comes over to the desk. Wipes her hands – and sees his phone on the desk. It's a really high-tech phone with remote control head piece.

Oooh, nice equipment, if you pardon the uh… (SPEAKS IN TO HEAD SET) ten-four, copy that, I'm on my way for the drop off.

A beat.

THINK "24"

FEMALE VOICE (FROM PHONE): Can I help with anything?

Miranda jumps.

Chicken leg flies out of her hand.

Doctor – Mrs Hawtry is here. And is everything OK?

MIRANDA: (TO ANTHONY) Can I?
(PRESSING PHONE TO TALK TO HER) Now listen carefully, we've taken Dr Hopkins hostage, we need half a million pounds and if someone comes in this room, we'll blow their brains out.

ANTHONY HOPKINS

PENNY: Hang on, did she say Mrs Hawtry? Excuse me. (TO PHONE) Hello. This is very important. Does Mrs Hawtry have a loud cardigan and a red gin nose?

194

FEMALE VOICE: Umm… yes.

PENNY: (TO PHONE) That will be all.
(TO MIRANDA) Mrs Hawtry is president of the parish mixed doubles. I cannot let her see me leaving a therapist's office.

Goes to the window. Checks it opens.

We'll have to climb out of the window at the end. She's the one who saw you buying the *Guardian*. That was embarrassing enough. I will not have it going around the tennis club that we've got issues.

MIRANDA: We don't. You've got issues.

Rhythm

PENNY: Excuse me, who was the one who presented three chocolate willies at the harvest festival. Let's not start.

MIRANDA: Fine.

Miranda hulas to the sofa. They sit down.

Miranda gets her phone and sends a text.

Penny looks at her watch.

A beat.

She looks at the phone.

Oh no (TO CAMERA IN A PANIC). I've sent the text I was going to send to Stevie, about Mum, to Mum.

Penny's phone gets a text.

Ah.

She dives to Penny's bag.

PENNY: What are you doing?

Penny reaches in her coat pocket and gets her mobile out.

Looks at text.

PENNY: Oh, it's a text from you. (READS IT) Stuck with Mum. Hell on earth. Prepare many drinks.

Miranda looks panicked to camera.

Anthony looks intrigued.

ANTHONY: Interesting.

MIRANDA: Doesn't mean anything does it? Mothers are just annoying. For no real reason. 'Oh darling you've got a new coat'. Annoying. Don't know why. I love you. (PATS PENNY'S ARM) Nothing personal.

PENNY: (BEAT) So Doctor, tell me, are you married?

MIRANDA: Annoyed again. (CROSS) You're clearly asking on my behalf.

PENNY: (CROSS) I'm simply making conversation. (BEAT) And he's a very handsome man in a very highly paid profession.

MIRANDA: (MORE HET UP) I knew it, you see this is exactly the kind of thing...

PENNY: (CROSS) No, no I can explain. When you have a daughter who has never had boyfriends...

MIRANDA: I've had boyfriends.

Thank you Georgia for that gag. Perfect for Patricia & Penny

PENNY: How many times, being flashed at does not constitute a relationship. She needs a little bit of help.

MIRANDA: I don't need help thank you. And the people you set me up with are ridiculous. (TO ANTHONY) No offence, I don't mean you. You're lovely just not in a kind of 'phwaaoor take me' kind of a way. Sorry I mean I'm sure lots of people look at you and go 'phwaaoor take me now'. I'm more kind of 'ummm'. Sorry I mean the other people you try and set me up with.

Poor MARK HEAP - HA!

Anthony is writing in his pad.

PENNY: Now look what you've done.

MIRANDA: What I've done?

He puts his pad down.

ANTHONY: Nothing to worry about.

He smiles at them.

They smile back.

A pause.

Penny gets her phone out, starts texting.

Miranda's phone gets a text.

MIRANDA: Oh it's from you.

Penny winks at her.

(READING THE TEXT) He's a bit smug isn't he?

197

PENNY: (TO ANTHONY COVERING UP) He… being a friend of ours…

MIRANDA: Yes… Japanese. Our Japanese friend, is a bit smug.

ANTHONY: So you were just thinking about your friend. He… what's his surname?

PENNY: Oh umm…

MIRANDA: He.

ANTHONY: He?

MIRANDA: He he? He's a right laugh. (LAUGHS) *Worryingly proud of this joke. Hee Hee*

PENNY: And I suddenly thought I must tell Miranda how smug He He is.

ANTHONY: Right… but with slightly strange grammar…

PENNY: That's how we say things. Miranda's being a bit silly today, isn't Miranda? As a random example. Good that's settled.

ANTHONY: As long as you're aware that I know you meant me, and not your friend He He. *Can't wait to hear Mark say that. Gosh, he's BRILLO PADS*

MIRANDA: I don't know where you get these things from? Do you need to see a therapist? Are you always thinking people think you're smug behind your back?

PENNY: He's paranoid. Classic case. I'm going to write this down in my note pad.

MIRANDA: Oh me too.

Penny and Miranda get out their note pads.

In fact, actually, role play. I think if you sit here.

Miranda sits at the desk, he sits on the sofa. Miranda takes her note pad, stares at him. He crosses his legs. Miranda writes furiously.

PENNY: Ooh yes yes yes.

MIRANDA: I'm sure that would help you a lot because you've clearly got some issues.

PENNY: (LOOKING AT HIS PHOTOS) Is this your father?

ANTHONY: Yes it is.

Penny sits on the side of the desk and puts a pair of Anthony's glasses at the end of her nose.

PENNY: Um interesting that you put it on your desk.

MIRANDA: Mmmm. Interesting.

PENNY: Mmmm. Interesting.

MIRANDA: Mmmmm.

PENNY: Mmmmm.

MIRANDA: Mmmmm.

ANTHONY: I know what you're doing. You're trying to put the focus on me because you're panicking that you've revealed too much about yourselves.

MIRANDA: You haven't got us pegged.
(TO CAMERA) He's totally got us pegged.

Looking at the shelf.

Oh hello, CD player – on pause. What have you been listening to?

She presses play. It's 'Alone' by Heart. It's at the slow part... Can't wait. *LOVE that ballad.*

PENNY: Oh now. This. Speaks. Volumes.

MIRANDA: A love ballad eh?

Miranda and Penny start dancing.

It goes to the chorus and Penny and Miranda do air guitar/drums.

*Miranda changes the track. It's 'I've Had The Time Of My Life'
from Dirty Dancing*

MIRANDA: Oh, fabulous… This is the best CD EVER!

Penny and Miranda start singing. We then go in to a fantasy.

We see Gary, in the black outfit Swayze wore in the film.

*A spotlight goes on Gary and Miranda, like in the film and they start the dance.
They do 10/15 seconds of the dance.*

Then we see Penny (in a different outfit, sitting at the back of the room).

PENNY: Of course you learned to dance from me.

MIRANDA: (FURIOUS) No I didn't!

Miranda turns off the CD player

MIRANDA: The only thing I get from you is a feeling of failure, guilt,
and very large feet.

PENNY: Where's this coming from? And we tried to get you to swim
competitively to make the most of the natural flippers God gave you.
No luck there either.

MIRANDA: Oh well I'm sorry, I'm glad I've been such a massive disap-
pointment to you.

Grabs a scotch egg.

PENNY: Look if you are going to eat, eat some fruit...

MIRANDA: Fatist. She took me to overeaters anonymous once, it's true.

With food in her mouth.

Totally unnecessary.

I always get weirdly nervous eating & acting

PENNY: I can explain... Belinda was showing off that Tilly had issues, so I said that you did.

ANTHONY: Well it seems the lies we tell end up in a therapy session of one kind or another.

PENNY: (REALLY ANNOYED) No, both the occasions to which you refer were entirely Miranda's problems.

MIRANDA: (FURIOUS) You're the one who gets me in to these scrapes. You do!

PENNY: You can pin all you want on me, but from what you've heard over the last half an hour, it doesn't take a genius to work out that Miranda's a bit odd, isn't Miranda?

Penny and Miranda argue at each other – top of their voices, we can hardly hear what they are saying lots of 'disappointed', 'can't take you anywhere', 'killed my dog', 'find a boyfriend', 'we weren't meant to be doing a session', 'people can probably hear this', 'you told him x', 'you told him y', 'that's why we turned your room in to a jacuzzi', 'i'll tell your father', 'don't bring dad in to this' etc.
It reaches a crescendo.

They stop.

A beat.

Anthony picks up his pad and starts really writing.

Has another thought, turns the page, keeps writing.

Puts the notebook down. And smiles at them.

They fake-smile back.

PENNY: (WHISPERS) We've got to get that notebook. It doesn't look like

shorthand now. Follow me. Pincer movement. We'll go commando.

MIRANDA: (TO CAMERA) Let's hope she doesn't know what that really means.

Penny & Miranda in sync, reunited

Penny approaches the desk and sits on the far side with the note pad behind her.

PENNY: (FLIRTING) So Anthony, if I may um… what else do you have in your CD collection?

During this she beckons Miranda.

Miranda crawls to near the desk and Penny flicks the note pad for Miranda to catch.

ANTHONY: Give me my pad back!

Anthony makes a grab for it, but Miranda whisks it away.

MIRANDA: Ooh I have it now, so what does it say? Dad – new toaster. Mum – garden knee pad. Don't forget presents from the pets. This is a Christmas list.

Miranda turns the page. It's a sketch of a cat.

PENNY: You drew a cat.

ANTHONY: Well, that's the end of the session. Would you like to book another appointment?

PENNY AND MIRANDA: No!!!

PENNY: (FLICKING THROUGH PAD) What's this shorthand bit?

ANTHONY: Just some initial thoughts at the top of the session.

MIRANDA: And what does it say — I can't wait to draw a kitten?

ANTHONY: Well actually it says…

Takes the pad, looks at shorthand and translates.

Mother and daughter. Mother's protective instinct has become dominating, fuelled by fear of how she is perceived by outer world. Daughter seeks mother's guidance and approval as she has yet to find her own voice.

Miranda and Penny stare at him.

A long silent pause.

MIRANDA / PENNY: Absolute rubbish…

They start gathering their stuff.

PENNY: I think he's nutty himself.

MIRANDA: Driven wholly by money.

PENNY / MIRANDA: Two hundred pounds?!

PENNY: Obsessed with his father.

MIRANDA: Only listens to love ballads. Very odd. In fact… I think one more before we go please doctor… hit it.

Chorus of 'This Thing Called Love' comes on.

They start dancing.

Anthony joins in.

GREAT TOON!

Caption: you have been watching.

Miranda Hart. Waves.

Patricia Hodge. Waves.

Mark Heap waves.

Tom Ellis pops his head in the door, waves, and pops out again.

They start heading out of the window.

Miranda suddenly remembers her trousers. Goes back, grabs them and puts them

over her shoulders, one leg on each side.

Suddenly a policeman knocks and comes in purposefully.

POLICEMAN: Is everything all right in here? Someone thought there might be a hostage situation…

He sees Miranda and Penny half way out of the window looking suspicious.

Miranda tosses one trouser leg round her neck like a scarf.

POLICEMAN: Hold on. It's you! The ice-cream child-catcher lunatics.

PENNY/ MIRANDA: (POINTING TO EACH OTHER**)**
It's her, she's mad.

We freeze on Miranda and Penny pointing at each other in the window.

Roll credits with 'This Thing Called Love' playing.

We don't normally freeze - see what it looks like in the edit. Like the concept for this ending.

208

Series Two, Episode Five
Behind the Scenes Tit-Bits

🎬 At 4 p.m. on day one of rehearsals I rushed home and was sick as a dog all night. Patricia then had to rehearse on her own all the next day. So I only had half of Wednesday and Friday to rehearse. It was fly by the seat of your pants.

🎬 To write the episode I spent some time at my parents' house and wandered around their sitting room one day acting as if I was wandering around a therapist's office, bored, as the character. I picked up lots of ornaments and played with them – my parents quietly thinking I had gone mad. The Russian dolls and the dancing flower pot that ended up in the script and on the TV both came from my parents' sitting room.

🎬 I have never seen Patricia Hodge nervous until the night of this recording. We both felt the pressure because if the audience didn't go with it, we had no back up. It was just us.

🎬 The first set piece that happened was when the tap got stuck on the water cooler and we were looking around for receptacles to catch the flowing water with. We had never done this before we filmed. Patricia is basically laughing the whole way through and

my performance became totally manic as I was determined to get it in the can.

The moment when I had to spill chicken on Mark Heap who played the therapist will go down as the luckiest bit of comedy as it landed perfectly – with no planning – on his wrist. *And* I managed not to laugh. I don't know how.

I love the fact that I made Patricia do air guitar to a rock ballad. A career high for us all!

We filmed the *Dirty Dancing* scene –Tom and I grabbed Craig Revel-Horwood in the BBC corridor as he was doing *Strictly* that Saturday. He gave us some tips. We cut the sequence in edit for time. No one will ever see it!

Certificate Of Achievement

This is to certify that .... irrelevantly,
but beautifully and with commitment, galloped in the following places:

Hospital ward

Church aisle at a christening

Church aisle at a wedding

Church aisle on any occasion

School corridor (particularly if you are the headmistress/master)

Down the beach before plunging into the sea

Diving board

Train platform

Into a job interview

Into No. 10 if you are a cabinet member

Miranda x

Founder

The Dinner Party

· · ·

Ah and we are in to Series Three. Writing-wise I am slightly more relaxed, the pressure is off a little. The tricky second album I got away with — phew. Although now I hear they want to move the show to BBC 1. Oh dear, let's not think about that. Let's just try and enjoy these characters and not get quite so het up about it all. What Series Three gave me, which I am very grateful for, was the chance to focus on the relationships between the characters, and get more emotional with them. Well as emotional as a studio audience sitcom can. Miranda was gaining more confidence. It was time to see her as part of a couple and get her a boyfriend. It was time to develop Stevie and Tilly more and further Miranda and Gary's feelings. I felt it was time to get them together. I get irritated watching will-they-won't-theys and if I am invested in one, then I can't take too much before I am just desperate to see them kiss. Romantic at heart. So although the audience had seen Miranda and Gary kiss, they had only ever seen it in Miranda's fantasy. Never for real. Series Three Episode Six would be the time. But I had to keep them apart until the final episode of the series and the only way to do that was to have them date other people. Which felt ripe for comedy — jealousy is always funny. Plus you get the universally recognisable jokes of how to behave at the beginning of a relationship and a woman's fear of never feeling like a good or impressive enough girlfriend. So what were the two hardest situations in the early stages of a relationship? My first and final thoughts were meeting their parents and having a dinner party. I was settled. This was going to be the dinner party episode.

I now wish I had done another bottle episode and just had a dinner party as a whole. Until I started writing it I didn't realise what fun I could have with it. But by then I had story-lined another episode in the series just set in the flat with Miranda and Penny ill in bed, so needed to stick with what I had. At least it meant we just got the best bits of a dinner party scene. It was one of my favourite scenes to film. And every single time in rehearsals we all completely fell apart – for a long time – when Stevie's fake boyfriend Norman, played brilliantly by Joe Wilkinson, said the line, after an awkward pause, 'I shat myself once'. So childish. But the way he delivered it was so brilliant and there were tears of laughter every time. Such a wonderful feeling, doubled up laughing around actors and friends you love. And luckily guest actor Tim Pigott-Smith, who was playing the boyfriend's father, found it equally funny. I was concerned he might think us all certifiable and ring Equity to get social services to the rehearsal room immediately.

This episode also gave me the following line, when Miranda gives up and refuses to conform to societal pressure any more. It shows she is gaining confidence and more and more becoming her own person. A celebration of a woman coming in to her own. It is also the nub of my on-screen persona (and a bit of the off screen one too).

Right, that's it! I drop the gauntlet. For the last two days I've tried to be a grown up but I have no interest in abiding by the adult rulebook. I want to do fun things that make me happy which by the way, for the record, include making vegtapals. Meet Mr Butternut. (GETS OUT MR BUTTERNUT) You might call me a child. Good. For if adults had even the slightest in-the-moment joy of a child then frankly the world would be a better place.

Good old alter ego!

INT. MIRANDA'S SITTING ROOM

Miranda is sitting in her armchair.

MIRANDA: (TO CAMERA) Well, bonjour to vous! That's the sort of sophisticated patter you'll get from a woman who's still got a boyfriend! Though elegance in the world of romance eludes me.

EXT. COUNTRYSIDE (FLASHBACK)

Miranda and Mike are walking along hand in hand. They come across a gate. Mike jumps effortlessly over it. He's about to turn and help Miranda but sees a bird.

MIKE: Oh, wow, look. A robin, lovely.

Miranda after a struggle manages to sit elegantly on top of the gate. Suddenly it swings open and tips her head into the bushes behind; she holds on to a branch of a tree and then kind of catches the gate back so when it swings shut she's elegantly sitting on top when he turns around.

INT. MIRANDA'S SITTING ROOM

MIRANDA: (TO CAMERA) But I'm proving myself a good lady woman for Mike.

INT. MIRANDA'S KITCHEN

Miranda in the kitchen with oven gloves.

PENNY: (OOV) Pssst...

Miranda goes to the window. We see Penny at the top of a ladder. She slides a lasagne in. Miranda puts it in the oven. Penny disappears. Mike enters. Miranda takes it out of the oven and puts it on the table.

INT. MIRANDA'S SITTING ROOM

MIRANDA: (TO CAMERA) Well, I don't want to lose him, he's great. But Operation Maintain Dignity means the suppressed silliness bursts out at inappropriate moments.

INT. YOGA CLASS (FLASHBACK)

YOGA TEACHER: Now close your eyes, breathe in and out. Relaxed. Peaceful and calm, and open your ey...

Could add Stevie in this scene. And M could be eating biscuits during yoga class – see what it looks like on camera

As the teacher says this Miranda crawls over
and comes nose to nose with the teacher.

The teacher opens her eyes and screams.
The whole class screams.

INT. MIRANDA'S SITTING ROOM

MIRANDA: (TO CAMERA) But generally I'm sophisticated girlfriend personified. I know this because a) I now own a pashmina and b) I've stopped giggling when people say sausage. (GIGGLES)

OPENING TITLES & MUSIC

INT. FLAT

Miranda is wearing an aertex shirt, zip up hoodie and culottes.
Stevie comes in with some papers. We now see the flat is a tip. Food cartons, fruit
friends, DVDs, trashy magasines, a standing swing ball.

STEVIE: Can you sign these? Oh, look at this place! Do you know, one night without Mike and the real you explodes.

MIRANDA: Well I'm not ready for him to know I make fruit friends and new vegtapals. Meet Mr Butternut. (HOLDS HIM UP)

STEVIE: Oh hello to you! (WAVES)

MIRANDA: I don't want that to put him off.

STEVIE: And what are you wearing?

MIRANDA: I happen to be sporting an elasticated culotte.

Oh Lordy what are these going to look like. LEGS OUT

STEVIE: Because you're a PE teacher from 1987?

MIRANDA: Cos I've got nothing else to wear. Washing machine's broken. Do you want a round of swing muffin?

STEVIE: Of course.

MIRANDA: Good luck!

Miranda swings muffin round and she and Stevie try to eat it as it passes.

MIKE: (OOV) Hello?

MIRANDA: Oh! It's Mike.

They rush to tidy.

Glee box set! Hide it!

Miranda throws the DVD to Stevie. Stevie throws her a modern art book to replace it.

STEVIE: Modern art!

MIRANDA: Nice.

STEVIE: Fruit friends! Fruit friends!

Miranda holds the bin. Stevie sweeps the fruit friends in

MIKE: (COMING IN) My taxi was going past and I just…

Miranda kisses him and indicates to Stevie to hide swing ball.

Miranda throws Mr Butternut to Stevie.

MIRANDA: Oh, I've missed you!

MIKE: Oh! Well I've, I've missed you too, I just came to get a glimpse really, I...

MIRANDA: I'll come down. (TO STEVIE) Pass my pashmina.

STEVIE: (SHAKING HER HEAD) No.

MIRANDA: It's my chic look!

Stevie passes it but we reveal Mr Butternut was underneath it.

MIKE: What? What's that?

MIRANDA: That is Stevie's.

STEVIE: Yeah, it's mine well it's my friend's. I'm looking after it whilst she's away, she didn't want to leave him in a kennel.

Miranda stares at Stevie. Mike looks confused.

INT. SHOP

Stevie is working. Miranda snaps toy in Stevie's face.

STEVIE: Ow!

MIRANDA: Do you want to play a game?

STEVIE: I'm working.

Miranda snatches pen.

MIRANDA: Oh come on, we could play 'What cereal am I?' Or 'Can we fit Stevie in a pillowcase?'

Let's try that with Sarah!!!

Miranda moves awkwardly arranging her pants.

Oh sorry, oh. My pants have gone (MOUTHS) northwards. Specifically north-north-east. Sorry. (TO CAMERA) Sorry.

Miranda walks weirdly and pulls pants out of bottom.

STEVIE: Urh, this is a public space!

MIRANDA: Sorry but I washed this last pair of pants in the dishwasher, and it sort of melted them. (OFF STEVIE'S LOOK) It was resourceful! Oh dear, no. It's getting really uncomfortable now actually.

A male customer walks in.

I'm going to have to take my pants off. (TO CUSTOMER)
Sorry sir, I didn't see you and immediately think I must take my pants off.
I'm not being lewd. Do excuse me. (TO CAMERA) Excuse me.

She goes to the kitchen area to change.

(OOV) Oh! No, I'm not sure about this going commando business. Oh no,
that feels wrong.

Stevie serves the customer.

STEVIE: I'm so sorry.

Miranda comes out.

MIRANDA: I'm a culotte incident away from moonery. (TO CUSTOMER)
Careful!

Customer exits.

STEVIE: How you think you're fit for the adult world of relationships
is beyond me.

MIRANDA: For that statement I find myself begging your pardon.

STEVIE: You're pretending to be someone you're not when you're with
Mike, then one night without him, you're a child again and the notion of
not wearing pants is hilarious. Just popping your maturity on the end
of my flagpole.

MIRANDA: You're just jealous Miss Singletepots! I'm a functioning adult
in a mature relationship.

Penny enters carrying linen.

PENNY: Darling, I've got your bed sheets. I ironed the *Knight Rider* duvet because David Hasselhoff was looking peculiar.

STEVIE: All Penny does is sort out your life.

PENNY: Excuse me Little Miss Oompa Loompa. I have a very busy life. I'm having work done on my kitchen. There are lunches, rotas. This week I'm on the rota for Rotary. I only did these because Miranda has to find a new plumber.

INT. FLAT (FLASHBACK)

Miranda lets a plumber in.

MIRANDA: It's just down 'ere guvnor, mate, me friend, alright? D'you want a brew? Jestive?

Plumber looks under the sink showing his crack.

PLUMBER: OK love, well let's just quickly seal this crack shall we.

Miranda takes tape out of his bag and gaffers his crack.

THIS COULD BE REALLY EMBARRASSING TO FILM! — tell casting director to tell actors exactly what it will involve.

INT. SHOP

MIRANDA: Right, I'm to have a mature adult day about town, fully commando.

Zips up top pointedly.

Actually I'm beginning to enjoy the freedom now.

PENNY: (GOING) Oh it's fabulous! I've been pantless since…

MIRANDA: Don't say this…

PENNY: I skinny dipped with Christopher Plummer-ed-me-thrice. Such fun!

Penny exits.

NO ONE GETS THIS. AM STILL GOING WITH IT.

MIRANDA: (TO CAMERA) I'll never recover. (OPENS DOOR) Ooh! (COMES BACK IN) That's breezy! How do you negotiate the frozen food aisles? (GIGGLES) Serious woman. (GRABS PASHMINA; EXITS) (OOV) Oooh! (GIGGLES)

INT. RESTAURANT

Gary is working. Chris and Alison are with a buggy, stressing about their toddler. Miranda strides in.

MIRANDA: (TO A DINER) I'm not wearing any pants. Enjoy your meatballs. Hi Gary. Hi Rose.

GARY: Hey.

ALISON: (ANGRILY) Where did you put the muslins Papa Bear?

MIRANDA: What's going on?

GARY: I was meant to be babysitting for Chris and Alison but I've got this urgent loan application I've got to fill out.

ROSE: Tell her. He's buying the restaurant!

MIRANDA: Wow, that's so exciting, Gary!

ROSE: Congrats babe.

GARY: Thanks darling (KISSES ROSE).

ROSE: See you later. (EXITS)   ↖ M WOULD GRIMACE AT THAT.

ALISON: You're sure you can't help us, Gary?

MIRANDA: Well hello? Babysitter.

GARY: Well hello, responsibility.

MIRANDA: Hello, rude.

CHRIS: We're, we're having a little bosom leakage.

MIRANDA: Oh, still breastfeeding?

In my mind their toddler is called Raymond

CHRIS: Well nothing beats mother's latte.

Miranda does a puke face.

GARY: So, good news – Miranda's offered to babysit.

ALISON: Oh. Well. We're desperate. It's only a couple of hours. It's a hospital appointment.

CHRIS: She's got to have a scrape.

MIRANDA: Oh, right, OK, now that's the kind of word you should mouth, alright? (SHE DEMONSTRATES) 'Scrape'.

CHRIS: We want to try for another.

ALISON: We *might* try for another. Only I can speak for my vagina.

MIRANDA: Why? Why? (THEY STARE AT HER)
(SINGS) Why Delilah? Wah, wah, wah, wah, wah, wah, wah!

ALISON: (TO CHILD) You're going to have fun with Auntie Miranda.
(TO MIRANDA) We've booked a music session at the soft play centre.
So, nappies, wipes, spare wipes, Mr Boo Boo. (HANDS A TEDDY OVER)

CHRIS: Now come on, dumpling! (THEY LEAVE)

225

GARY: Thank you. You're a lifesaver.

Goes to kiss Miranda on the cheek, they miss and nearly go for lips.

MIRANDA: Ooh, nearly snogged there!

N.B. Need to keep spark alive for G & M

They laugh. A moment.

MIRANDA: Right, OK. Sophisticated lady coming through.

Miranda's pashmina gets caught in the buggy wheels and she's brought to ground.

My pashmina's got stuck in... I think it's stuck...

She crawls towards the door.

INT. SOFT PLAY CENTRE

In the corner is a music session. The teacher is an over-the-top musical theatre type and sings even when she'd normally be speaking.

PLAYGROUP: (SINGING) Old MacDonald had a farm... E-I-E-I-O...

TEACHER: (SINGS) It's nearly time to finish up, so on to the final round...

MIRANDA: (TO CAMERA) (SINGING) She sings everything, it's totally brilliant!

TEACHER: (SINGS) And on that farm he had a...

She turns to Miranda.

MIRANDA: My turn? Err, Dolphin! Out of the box. With a... (MAKES A WEIRD NOISE) here and a (CLICKS) there, here a (NOISE), there are (NOISE) everywhere a (NOISES).

TEACHER: Right, I think we'll end it there!

INT. SOFT PLAY AREA

Miranda running around the soft play centre. Ventures into the climbing tunnel.

MIRANDA: (SHOUTING AT KIDS) Move up, move up!

She gets stuck. We see children stuck behind her, piling up in the tunnel.

MIRANDA: Oh, oh me back's gone. Kids backing up. Oh you stink!

The teacher has crawled up and faces her.

TEACHER: (SINGING BRIGHTLY) Somebody looks a bit stuck.

They are both sitting at the top of a bumpy slide

TEACHER: This is the only way down.

MIRANDA: But my back. I can't and I'm scared. I'm sorry I just…

The teacher suddenly pushes Miranda who slides down screaming.
The toddlers all follow. Miranda lands in the ball pool.

Oh, I can't – ooh! Oh my back! Get me out of here…

INT. OSTEOPATH TREATMENT ROOM

The osteo room is formal, with massage table with roll of paper on it. There is a lit candle, calming pictures and a large standing skeleton. The osteo (Valerie – a man) is standing behind Miranda looking and feeling her lower back. He is 60s, confident, high status, got a slight London accent, and is wearing a toupee.

VALERIE: Yes, yes, I – yes I think we ought to be able to ease that. So if you'd like to get down to your bra, bra and vest and pants, then I'll pop back in a moment.

He exits. Miranda goes behind screen.

She takes off her shirt so is in slip and bra. She takes off trousers and then realises...

MIRANDA: (GASPS) No pants!

VALERIE: (OOV) Yes, twenty milligrams of Voltarol should do the trick.

Miranda grabs the paper from the couch.

(OOV) And tell her that I'll speak to her when I've seen my patient.

MIRANDA: Oh my!

Valerie re-enters.

VALERIE: Right.

Turns to miranda. We reveal Miranda in the paper pants. Valerie gets another roll of paper to put on his couch.

MIRANDA: Oh right! You do need the paper on the couch. I presumed it was there for origami. Hence origami pants slash nappy. Has anyone ever done you a swan or...?

VALERIE: No you're the first patient who's done origami.

MIRANDA: Well it's a happy day for us both then isn't it?

VALERIE: (LOOKS BLANK) So if you'd like to lie face up on the couch please.

MIRANDA: As the osteo said to the patient! No? OK.

He begins to manipulate Miranda's back and gets quite close.

Ooh! Hello! Intimate isn't it? We'll have to become engaged after this sir.

Suddenly sees his wig slipping.

MIRANDA: Wig! (TO CAMERA) Wig!   How will we do this?

Miranda kind of blows at the wig to try and push it back up. He sees. She turns it into pout and kind of blows kisses.

VALERIE: And if you'd like to lie on your side please?

He leans on her and does a crunch in a compromising position.

MIRANDA: Oooh did we just consummate our engagement?

VALERIE: And on to your back. One final stretch, OK.

*Valerie pushes her knees down on to chest. She does a big fart
and blows out the candle.*

Miranda clocks camera.

*And How will we do this?!
Really want to be able to
do all this scene in front
of audience & not have to
prerecord it. Be too hard
without hearing laughs.*

INT. SHOP

Miranda comes downstairs wearing her 'Where's Miranda?' outfit.

STEVIE: Oh, good day to you. 1. Why are you wearing your Where's
Miranda? outfit? And b) How was your mature day about town?

MIRANDA: 1. I only have this left to wear, the washing machine is still
broken. And b) I got stuck in a tunnel in a soft play centre, did my back in,
went pantless to an osteopath where I farted and blew out a candle.

STEVIE: (STARES) I don't...

MIRANDA: I know. I know. And instead of getting over it all like a normal
thirty-something with a glass of red and a leaf through *Tatler*, last night
I got a felt tip pen and decorated my breasts as Jedward. Mike is going to
realise I'm a nonsense and dump me.

*Thank you Georgia for that
joke – a delightful image*

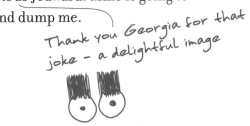

STEVIE: Then sire, I throw down the 'It's Time To Grow Up And Do Without Mummy' gauntlet.

MIRANDA: Well sire, I pick up your gauntlet. With such verve and vigour, I smash it about your little tiny face.

Mike enters.

MIKE: Hey Quirky!

MIRANDA: Hi!

They kiss.

MIKE: Listen, about tonight I just had a call from Dad, he's really down so I said I'd go out with him.

MIRANDA: No worries.

MIKE: Well actually he asked about finally meeting you.

MIRANDA: Ooh, that's a step I'm not sure if…

STEVIE: (SUDDENLY SHOUTS) Gauntlet!

MIRANDA: Gauntlet! Sorry. Yes, good, no I would like to meet my boyfriend's father. Bring him round, I'll cook.

Nods to Stevie. Stevie positive reaction.

MIKE: Great. Bit nervous. With previous girlfriends there's always been a bit of a culling.

MIRANDA: Culling?

MIKE: He's, he's particular.

MIRANDA: Is he? Good. (TO CAMERA) Help.

Penny walks in.

PENNY: I've stitched your bra.

Miranda pushes Penny over.

MIRANDA: Bra, bra, bra, bra, bra bra-bar-ran. Is how excited I am about tonight. (KISSES MIKE) See you later.

Mike exits. Miranda picks Penny up.

Sorry, Mother, sorry it's just I am with gauntlet and from now on I take all adult tasks on. For tonight I cook for my boyfriend's father.

MIRANDA & STEVIE: Sire!

PENNY: It's for Mike's father? Err, no that's fine, that's fine. Very happy not to get involved, sire. Bye Miranda, live well.

They hug.

(WHISPERS TO MIRANDA) Wine glasses not tumblers and use the crockery your aunt left you.

STEVIE: Penny! Go!

She separates them.

MIRANDA: Which one's that?

PENNY: The flowery one.

MIRANDA: No, which one's crockery? Plates or spoons?

PENNY: Oh help us all! Bye, darling.

Exits.

MIRANDA: Bye, Mummy.

STEVIE: Oh, it's for your own good.

Stevie goes into the kitchen. Penny pops back in.

PENNY: Red wine meat, white wine fish and if in doubt, Delia.

STEVIE: (COMING BACK FROM THE KITCHEN) Oi! (TO MIRANDA) I knew you'd never do it 'mature relationship'.

MIRANDA: Oh well, now, I have had enough of this doubting little Miss and Mrs Doubtfire. Yeah. (SNAPS HER FINGERS)
Tonight I shall have a couples' dinner party and without your help I shall have a soiree with home-cooked fayre and good crockery (TO CAMERA) which is plates. And there shall be Bublé on the stereo and I won't even laugh at the name Bublé. (LAUGHS) It's got boob in it! Stevie, if you manage to get a boyfriend by tonight, do come.

She goes upstairs.

INT. FLAT, AFTERNOON

Miranda is in the kitchen. A range of ingredients neatly laid out.

MIRANDA: Right ingredients, hello to you alfalfa. I thought you were a llama but a hearty welcome. Right let's do this, it can't be that hard!

INT. FLAT, EVENING

A few hours later. The kitchen is in total chaos. Miranda is cross and stressed.

MIRANDA: (TO CAMERA) It's really hard! At one point I was told to skiffle carrots. Skiffle! Am I to play them a percussive instrument and dance for them? I confused tsp with tsbp. Trying to do a salmon terrine starter. (SHE TRIES TO WRAP CLING FILM AROUND HER RIDICULOUS LOOKING TERRINE) Who can strike clean a piece of cling film? I was going to do crepe suzette for pudding but um.

We see three burnt pancakes on the ceiling. She opens a cupboard.

Penis pasta? What's that doing there? That's not funny to eat in your thirties. I see only one option.

Recall from Series One

INT. SUPERMARKET

Miranda rushing around. She stumbles upon a salmon terrine.

MIRANDA: (HOLDS IT UP) All hail! A terrine. Even potatoes! Why do we bother cooking? Why?

WOMAN: I'm doing this fish pie for six and they'll never know.

MIRANDA & OTHER WOMEN: (AS A DITTY) Praise M&S putting food on our table, (OTHER SHOPPERS JOIN THEM) coz cooking drives us crazy, we're busy-slash-lazy. (TO CAMERA) Other upmarket food stores are available!

MIRANDA: Ladies, go. Decant in your own dishes and lie!

I should set an M & S campaign for this ! CALL AGENT !

They disband happily.

INT. FLAT

Gary, Rose and Penny have arrived. The terrine is on a chopping board in the kitchen. Miranda is wearing a dress, has an apron around her waist. Bublé is on. Gary and Rose are babysitting Chris and Alison's child and getting him ready for bed.

MIRANDA: Who has caused me a wonky throw?

GARY: Now are you sure you don't mind us babysitting? I'm really sorry I just have to make it up with Chris and Alison.

MIRANDA: Of course.

ROSE: (COMING IN FROM BEDROOM) Can I pop the baby monitor here?

PENNY: I am not interfering, darling. If I were I would say dab that stain off your dress. I'm saying nothing.

MIRANDA: Mother, this is soap because I hand washed it and I've called the plumber back. I am an in-control adult with my cocktail sausages.

The doorbell rings. She spills sausages. She takes a breath and opens the door. Stevie enters with a traffic warden (Norman).

STEVIE: This is my boyfriend, Norman. We've come for the dinner party.

MIRANDA: You have clearly just dragged a traffic warden off the street.

STEVIE: No, no we're seeing each other. (NORMAN GOES TO KISS HER)

Get off me.

Thanks Hadders & Joe for that idea.

Rose comes out of the bedroom.

ROSE: Babe, come and help me settle him.

GARY: Yeah, sure.

Miranda points at Norman the traffic warden.

MIRANDA: (TO STEVIE) Get this out!

MIKE: (OOV) Yes she bought the shop four years ago.

MIRANDA: Bum bummery! They're here. OK act normal, act normal.

They all act strangely, attempting normal.

No, more natural. More natural. Just…

They act stranger, ending in a weird pose.
Mike brings in his dad.

MIKE: Miranda, this is my father.

It's the osteopath from yesterday. Miranda stares.

Then clocks camera.

VALERIE: Well.

MIRANDA: Well.

VALERIE: Very nice to meet you, Miranda.

MIRANDA: Very nice to meet you too, Mr Jackford.

VALERIE: Call me Valerie.

MIRANDA: (LAUGHS) Yeah, good one, call me Derek!

MIKE: Dad's name is Valerie.

Penny puts her head in her hands.

MIRANDA: What's your mum called, Dave? (LAUGHS) Right, let me introduce you to my mother for tonight you are a Valerie Singleton if you...

MIKE: Dad, this is Penny.

MIRANDA: Stevie, osteopath, he was the osteopath!

STEVIE: No.

MIRANDA: (WHISPERING) Sir, um, could I take your coat?

She does. Valerie is flicking some keys.

Lovely, and your keys?

VALERIE: Or shall I throw them in a bowl?

Winks at Stevie. Stevie looks alarmed. As does everyone. A pause. Valerie bursts out laughing. Everyone fake laughs.

MIRANDA: It's a joke! (TO CAMERA) It's a joke!

MIKE: (TO MIRANDA) Sorry. You OK?

MIRANDA: Yes of course. Yes. Now, do sit down, let me plump a scatter cushion. Help yourself to sausages. Can I get you a warming glass o' rouge?

Mike and Valerie nod. Miranda goes to kitchen area. Penny and Stevie rush to her.

(TO CAMERA) I'm so getting culled!

PENNY: (POINTING AT VALERIE) Wig.

PENNY, MIRANDA & STEVIE: (WHISPERING TOGETHER) Wig, wig.

Valerie and Mike look round. They all wave. Miranda brings the drinks.

MIRANDA: There you go.

VALERIE: Oh thank you.

MIRANDA: Now do relax in my nibble and mingle zone.

She sits on the sofa arm nearest Mike.

A pause. ——— *Let's be as brave as we can with this pause*

ALL: (BEGIN TALKING OVER EACH OTHER)

Another pause.

GARY: (COMES OUT OF BEDROOM WITH ROSE, CARRYING A NAPPY) He's just done an explosive poo right up to his armpits.

VALERIE: Well on that note I think I'll leave. (BEAT)

Laughs.

Everyone sort of fake laughs.

MIRANDA: It was a joke, yeah! (TO CAMERA) was a joke.

Pause. LONG PAUSE

NORMAN: I shat myself once.

Miranda gives Stevie a disappointed look.

HOLD IT
TOGETHER HART.
MH

MIRANDA: Now let me just sort out my dessert. I've got syphilis.

Everyone stares. Miranda goes to kitchen. A pause. Miranda comes back from the kitchen with a fruit.

MIRANDA: I meant physalis. Physalis, physalis, the fruit, exotic fruit.
I have not got syphilis.

241

A beat. Valerie suddenly laughs.

(TO CAMERA) Laughter delay.

Now, you know what's for dessert, but for starter we're having a smoked salmon terrine and for main we shall be having lamb. So, the terrines, I'll just get them out. And the terrines. (LAUGHS) It's a joke about getting your breasts out instead of the terrines. One for you. (LEANS TOWARDS VALERIE) Nothing.

Be brave in waiting for the Valerie laugh

INT. FLAT

Everyone at the table with the terrines. Valerie clinks his glass.

VALERIE: Shall we say grace?

MIRANDA: Oh right.

STEVIE: Oh yes.

PENNY: Yes of course, we always do.

Miranda puts her hands in a prayer position, everyone follows. Valerie looks at Miranda who realises, at head of table, she should say grace.

could sing this bit too or overkill?

MIRANDA: Me? Right. Um. Lord, um we thank you for the music. The songs we're singing, and, um, we thank you for your bread of heaven, bread of heaven, feed me till I want no more. *Want no more!* Feed me till I want no more, so much, thank you very much to you God please, amen.

Everyone starts eating.

MIKE: Mmm!

GARY: It's really good!

PENNY: Delicious!

Miranda clocks camera.

VALERIE: What did you use?

MIRANDA: Oh, erm, well, skills, erm, utensils, terrine mix, terrine powder.

NORMAN: I think I've got a bit of pants in my terrine.

STEVIE: They'll be Miranda's. She had to wash them in the dishwasher.

MIRANDA: Right, excuse me whilst I check on my gravy.

Miranda crosses to the kitchen. She coughs loudly to cover up the sound of piercing the M&S film lid of the potatoes. We hear a cry from the monitor.

ROSE: I'll go.

She goes to the bedroom.

VALERIE: Are you thinking of having children, Miranda? All that dribbling and talking gibberish, you've got plenty in common.

A pause. He laughs.

MIKE: Dad!

Penny should be pretty pissed by now.

PENNY: Do you think you could do the laugh while you're making the joke? That way there won't be any false starts.

MIKE: I think she'd make a great mum.

PENNY: Well she's already got a (MOUTHED) very weak (LOUDLY) pelvic floor. Such fun!

STEVIE: Penny, why don't you tell us about the work you're having done?

VALERIE: Yes what are you having done? The crow's feet I can see.

PENNY: On my kitchen. On my kitchen you stupid old—

MIRANDA: Shall we play a game? (SINGS) Heads, shoulders, knees and toes, knees and toes...

Genuinely love this game. WRONG MH!

VALERIE: That's a kid's game!

MIRANDA: Yes, it's a ridiculous suggestion! I prefer dinner party convo. So, um, well, Norman, what do you do for a hobby?

NORMAN: I like to let kittens feed from my beard.

MIRANDA: Shall we play a game? I think we should play a game.

STEVIE: Let's play a game. Let's play a game. A game, let's play a game.

GARY: What about the Were-Game? You know, if you were going to be a were animal for one night like a, werewolf. What animal would you be?

PENNY: What, like Valerie would be a were-toupee?

ALL: (SINGS) Heads, shoulders, knees and toes, knees and toes...

INT. FLAT

A while later. Everyone more raucous. Miranda in the kitchen taking out the lamb.

MIRANDA: Lamb looks OK, I've made new gravy, I'm clawing it back.

Miranda drops the meat on the surface, it jumps on to the floor. No one notices.

MIRANDA: Oh! My meat's gone mobile. Oh hot! Five second rule. (SHE TRIES TO PICK IT UP; IT SLIPS OUT). Hot! Five second rule. (SHE TRIES TO PICK IT UP; IT SLIPS OUT) Hot! Five second rule. Oh!

She jumps and drops the meat straight out of the window.

PENNY: What is going on?

MIRANDA: My meat's gone mobile. Valerie thinks I'm insane. You're not helping.

PENNY: Now listen here, I like Mike and you are more than good enough for him. I do not like Valerie. I will not be dictated to by Stevie the crazed leprechaun and a man with a dead badger on his head. We stick together.

MIRANDA: Oh Mummy! Help me with a new main course. Oh, Mum! The microwave is about to go ping, I've put the M&S potatoes in there.

STEVIE: What are you two up to in there?

MIRANDA & PENNY: Nothing!

The microwave starts to beep. Miranda and Penny scream to cover up the noise. Everyone looks round.

MIRANDA: Sorry, we thought we saw a…

PENNY: Mouse.

GARY: What?

Gary jumps on a chair.

ROSE: Really babe?

PENNY: Oh, you need to man up. I am so pleased my daughter has moved on to your lovely son, Vanessa. *Really drunk by now*

ROSE: What do you mean moved on?

PENNY: She's had a thing for Gary for years.

MIRANDA & GARY: It wasn't really a thing.

MIKE: Well was it a thing or wasn't it a thing?

MIRANDA: Well, if you can call a couple of dates—

ROSE: You dated?

GARY: Well nothing ever really happened.

STEVIE: Oh tell me about it, on off, on off.

Miranda and Gary stare at her.

MIKE: And do you still want it to be on?

GARY & MIRANDA: No, no, no, no, no. No! *Try and say this as together as we can.*

We hear the baby cry. Rose gets up.

STEVIE: I'll give you a hand.

GARY: Rose.

Will that sound realistic/ believable?

They follow her. Penny goes too. Norman goes to the bathroom. We hear everyone next door on the baby monitor. Miranda, Valerie and Mike at the table in vision.

PENNY: (OOV) You are not doing Miranda any favours.

STEVIE: (OOV) She's on a losing streak with that Valerie.

PENNY: (OOV) Her first proper boyfriend and the father's got the personality of a self-service check out.

GARY: (OOV) Oh and that wig! It's like roadkill!

PENNY: (OOV) Yes well if Miranda gets desperate we can always grill that!

They all laugh. A pause.

STEVIE: (OOV) This monitor's on isn't it?

Slowly everyone comes back and sits down again in silence. We hear a very long pee from the bathroom.

MIRANDA & PENNY: Brazen wee. *Recall from Ep 5, S2 therapist office.*

Valerie gets up and goes to the kitchen with his glass.

MIRANDA: Sir, can I get you a drink? Would you like a tea, perhaps a chamomile?

PENNY: She's got a red bush.

MIRANDA: The tea, the tea!

A pancake from the ceiling lands on Valerie's head.

Sorry! I was trying crepe suzette earlier, sorry.

Helps him take it off. The wig comes away with the pancake. Miranda puts the pancake back on his head, realises, and gives him back the wig.

VALERIE: Right son, I've had enough of this. I don't care to come to a so-called dinner party to be insulted by your girlfriend's freaky friends and dysfunctional family.

PENNY: (DRUNK) Excuse me, my functional is not disfamily. We're not fysdunctional.

MIRANDA: Mr Jackford, I know I haven't portrayed myself well but I am a capable woman.

Let's try & do this in front of audience & not prerecord so can run it through – Keep actor's momentum going.

VALERIE: Then why is foam rising throughout your kitchen?

MIRANDA: Oh no! I put Fairy Liquid in the dishwasher. I am normal!

Plumber arrives.

PLUMBER: Hello? I'm only coming in if you don't wax my crack again, alright?

Penny puts pasta into a bowl.

VALERIE: Is that penis pasta?

MIRANDA: Right, that's it! I drop the gauntlet. For the last two days I've tried to be a grown up but I have no interest in abiding by the adult rulebook. I want to do fun things that make me happy which by the way, for the record, include making vegtapals. Meet Mr Butternut. (GETS OUT MR BUTTERNUT) You might call me a child. Good. For if adults had even the slightest in-the-moment joy of a child then frankly the world would be a better place.

YAY

Miranda whips out the terrine packaging.

MIRANDA: Oh! And the terrine? M&S.

ALL: (GASP)

ROSE: Well I bet you're glad your 'thing' with her is over now.

GARY: No. Miranda's my best friend, Rose, and I'm not gonna say what you want me to say, so if you can't handle that then, do you know what? It's over.

ROSE: Fine

She exits.

Penny does the EastEnders *theme tune intro, then laughs.*

VALERIE: Come on, Mike.

MIKE: No. I'm staying. (TO MIRANDA) These last two days I've been worried that you weren't who I thought you were because I was falling in love with you. Your ridiculous sense of humour and your smile and the way you bring me out of my boring shell and well, hearing what you just said I realised I have fallen in love with you. I love you, Quirky.

Miranda mouths aghast to camera.

Mike and Miranda kiss. Gary looks sad in the background.

Norman goes to kiss Stevie who pushes him away.

STEVIE: Get off!

MIKE: And do you know what I really want to do?

MIRANDA & MIKE: Foam fight!

They all play and dance to Billy Joel's 'River of Dreams'.

Think that's what the song is called. Has to be Billy Joel for M when she is on a high. OBVS

You Have Been Watching

Miranda Hart
Bo Poraj
Patricia Hodge
Sarah Hadland
Tom Ellis
Naomi Bentley
Tim Pigott-Smith

Series Three, Episode Three
Behind the Scenes Tit-Bits

🎬 I had a temperature of 103 filming this episode and had sick buckets in the wings in case. The show must go on.

🎬 The osteopath scene where I farted is based on a true story. I won't say who. Oh, OK. Me. But I never blew a candle out. Always take it to the next step for the sitcom.

🎬 I very rarely laugh when I write but I laughed out loud, on my own, to myself, in my kitchen, for far too long when I wrote the bit about being a dolphin and making dolphin noises in 'Old Macdonald Had a Farm' when I was looking after Chris and Alison's child at the soft play centre.

 This ended up randomly being the episode of guest appearances. Paul Kerensa, the writer, was the customer that I almost flashed at in the first shop scene. Sarah Hadland's mother (otherwise known as Beaky) was the woman who I flicked my pashmina at in the restaurant and told I was wearing no pants. And my sister (to the left of me) was the singing lady in the M&S scene.

Gary's Savoury Muffins

Who said muffins have to be a sweet? These scrumptious cheese & onion gems are great with soup.

Preparation

Preperation time: 15min Cooking time: 25min Total: 40min

1. Heat up the oven to 200°C/180°C fan (gas mark 6) and either line a 12 cup muffin tin with paper muffin cases or oil the tin itself.
2. Mix the flour, mustard powder, 1 tsp salt, 1/2 tsp pepper in a mixing bowl and stir in the cheese, spring onions and chives.
3. Whisk the milk, egg and oil and delicately fold this into the dry mix using a large spoon. Be sure to do this carefully and add the soft cheese to the final folds.
4. Spoon the mixture into the muffin cases or oiled tin.
5. Bake for 30 minutes or until slightly browned.

Ingredients

250g soft cheese ~~ NO!
150g cheddar cheese
284ml carton buttermilk mixed with 100ml whole milk
sunflower oil ^
1 1/2 tsp Mustard powder
1 bunch spring onions.
small bunch chives NO!
500g self raising flour
1 egg

life is full of enough disappointments Gary!

Queen of Words

Gary's Beetroot Cake

If you haven't yet tried it, discover the ridiculously moist wonders of this delicious beetroot cake.

this is a vegetable out of context Gary
There is no place for beetroot in cake!

Preparation

Preparation time: 15 min Cooking time: 45min Total: 1hr

1. Heat up the oven to 180°C/160°C fan (gas mark 4) and grease and line the bottom of a springform cake tin.
2. Use a sieve to sprinkle the sugar, baking powder, flour and cocoa into a large bowl.
3. Drain the beetroot and chop into small pieces. Place into a blender, crack in the eggs one at a time, then pour in the oil. Blend until the liquid is a pinky colour and smooth in texture.
4. Stir this mixture into the dry mixture and add the finely chopped dark chocolate. Pour this into the tin and bake for 45 mins.
5. Dust with icing sugar just before serving.

Ingredients

250g cooked beetroot
3 eggs
220ml sunflower oil
150g dark chocolate
1 1/2 tsp baking powder
60g unsweetened cocoa powder
170g plain flour
200g caster sugar
icing sugar

Why not sweetened?

Ridiculous Cake! What next Gary? Pea and ham sponge?!!

Three Little Words

I call this the farce episode. But most people call it the Gary Barlow episode.

I had met Gary when we did the Jubilee Concert together and to my great pleasure and surprise he said he was a big fan of the sitcom. I didn't immediately think there and then that I would like to get him in the show, but as I started thinking about this storyline I had the idea that Miranda got her own back on Stevie, who snogged Gary (Tom Ellis's Gary) by snogging someone Stevie really liked. It felt funny if it was two women going "you kissed MY Gary". So I thought of Gary Barlow. He agreed to do it when I emailed him months before and then a few weeks before production we weren't sure if he was going to be available. The story just wouldn't have been the same. We nearly asked Olly Murs at one point but somehow Stevie loving Gary Barlow made so much more sense and was utterly believeable. Not dissing Olly. Heavens no. Wouldn't do that. I am all about current popular tunes. I think at one point we were going to approach Ant McPartlin. I believe Stevie would have a love o' Ant. But I am very grateful that Gary Barlow bravely stepped forward. It made the farce come together at the end. The audience that night didn't know what had hit them. There was a gasp and then a massive scream. Brilliant. A great moment to be on a studio floor.

This was another episode I actually enjoyed writing. Two out of the eighteen! I knew exactly how I wanted it and it was as much of a fast paced farce as I could do on TV. My parents used to take me to all the Ray Cooney farces when I was younger so I had that theatrical farce influence, and I had always wanted to do it with the sitcom and now there was a story that served it. I remember having to explain to the director exactly the pace I wanted it to go at and I directed the actors a bit in rehearsal, because there was a particular rhythm I had written. It was probably the hardest show to rehearse. The number of times me, Sarah and Dominic Coleman, who played the shop customer embroiled in this story against his will, rehearsed our little Take That singing moments… If it wasn't 100 per cent precise it was never going to work.

I am very lucky in my director Juliet May, who trusts my vision of the show and can let me from time to time put my oar in and direct the performances. And I think this episode was our working relationship at its best. I never interfere with her technical side of the directing. That is, all the camera shots, angles and sizes. She may very rarely ask me what I think about a shot as regards serving a joke as best TV can. And on very few occasions I may ask to see a shot back if we are pre-recording it, or look at it when we are camera rehearsing on the day of the record. But those occasions are rare. We totally trust each other and I don't think there has been a single occasion where I have watched the show back in the edit and thought she messed up a joke or shot or didn't serve the show as best she could. When we first met I said I wanted it to be theatre on TV. Lots of full-length shots to see the physical comedy. Lots of movement in the performances. It makes it more challenging to do on the studio floor but it always serves the comedy more and makes it more interesting to watch. So I was not only lucky with the cast, but am eternally grateful to have found Juliet.

That's enough praise for her… back to me. Although actually can I just say how much I love Dominic Coleman. He was in an episode in Series One (Episode Five) as a customer who found himself getting sucked in to Miranda and Stevie's world as they asked his advice on how to deal with Penny. He then couldn't leave. And I always knew I wanted to write him back in to the show. His character and performance worked perfectly for a more farcical set up. Right that really is enough about others. Back to me and my farcey-pode, as I like to call it.

Miranda is making breakfast. There are two eggs with faces drawn on and parsley for hair. She has made spoon shaped toast to dip. 'Good Morning' is playing.

INT. FLAT

MIRANDA: (TO CAMERA, SINGING) Good morning, good morning! Sunbeams will soon smile through, good morning, good morning, (TO CAMERA) to you and you and you and you. Look, toast spoons! I'm feeling good about today, it's got a sort of frisson about it. So, news. Mike and I still together, all good, but when he tells me he loves me, I freak out, can't say it back.

EXT. RIVER (FLASHBACK)

Mike and Miranda are walking down the quayside.

MIKE: I love you.

MIRANDA: Oh well, well done and you're welcome and what a boost! (LAUGHS; PRETENDS HER HAND IS A FAN) It's a fan hand. Forsooth sir!

INT. FLAT

MIRANDA: (TO CAMERA) I need to workshop the issue with Stevie but we've fallen out. Apparently I've ignored her since having a boyfriend. Objection my lord! Although at disco karaoke finals.

INT. KARAOKE NIGHT (FLASHBACK)

Stevie as Jennifer Grey and Miranda as Patrick Swayze from the Dirty Dancing *film. They are dancing to 'I've Had The Time of My Life'.*

Miranda dances down the aisle briefly. She turns to Stevie. Stevie nods to go for the lift. Stevie runs towards Miranda, lifts off, Miranda sees Mike coming in, turns to wave and kiss him. Stevie flies past, out of frame. CANNOT WAIT TO FILM. Makes writing worthwhile. (Just)

INT. FLAT

MIRANDA: (TO CAMERA) What else to impart? Mum's having a tennis club dinner tonight. She doesn't want me there. Apparently I let her down last year. Sidebar m'lord!

INT. POSH DRINKS PARTY

Miranda is sitting on an elaborately laid table. A waiter passes with drinks.

MIRANDA: Oh I'll 'serve' drinks.

She gets a tennis racket and 'serves' glasses at people.

PENNY: I don't know who this woman is.

INT. FLAT

'Good Morning' is still playing.

MIRANDA: (TO CAMERA) Right! (STARTS DANCING) I declare this cheeky little day ready and open for the business we call life!

INT. RESTAURANT

The restaurant has had a refurb. Perhaps a slightly different feel. And decorations (cokeys grill sign gone). It still needs things doing. A shelf to be put up, there's a power drill on the bar, a table with candles/fairy lights that need distributing, maybe chairs in wrapping etc. Mike and Miranda are having breakfast. Mike has lots of papers, and his phone out on the table. Gary is busy and stressed.

MIRANDA: Oh Gary, look at you in your own restaurant.

MIKE: Are you renaming it?

MIRANDA: What, Gary's?

GARY: What's wrong with 'Gary's'?

MIKE: Well it's like a greasy spoon.

MIRANDA: Yeah it's like, it's like a chippy is 'Gary's', isn't it? Yeah. No, seriously, what are you calling it?

Gary shows the sign: 'Gary's'.

MIRANDA: No that's lovely, no that's perfect.

MIKE: It's very you.

MIRANDA: Manly, yeah.

GARY: Manly? Good because now manning up to put sign up.

MIRANDA: Good luck, man who gets nervous voting for *Strictly* and is scared of mice and geese?

GARY: It's the hissing. They hiss.

Stevie enters.

MIKE: Ah, morning Stevie, do you want to join?

STEVIE: (POINTEDLY TO MIRANDA) Fine on my own.

She struggles to get on a stool.

MIRANDA: Struggling to get on the stool, are we?

STEVIE: Pretending this isn't our second breakfast, are we? (MIRANDA LOOKS SHEEPISH) I won!

GARY & MIKE: Guys! I do not need this today.

MIKE: Our family dog, my dog, Daisy, might have to be put down.

GARY: But more importantly, hello, restaurant opening tonight?

MIKE: More importantly?

MIRANDA: OK, can we all just calm it please? Everyone seems at odds. Just calm.

Pause.

MIRANDA: Do you know what my favourite three little words are?

Mike looks hopeful.

All day breakfast.

GARY: I'm going to start doing it.

MIRANDA: Shut up! It's the best thing since sliced bread. It is sliced bread. Then it's toasted and an egg's popped on.

STEVIE: Mike, please ask your girlfriend, who loves you *so* much she…

MIKE: (OVER STEVIE) Well—

STEVIE: Ignores best friends, if she would for once share her pancakes?

Miranda gets up with a pancake and moulds it on to Stevie's face.
Mike gets up to take a call.

MIRANDA: (WHILST PUTTING PANCAKE ON STEVIE) Oh, sorry about this, oh no I really am sorry. I mean if I could stop I would.

Ask Sarah if this will be OK

STEVIE: Well that is it. I will show you how angry I am by my exit march. (FURIOUSLY MARCHES OUT) See my physical anger!

MIRANDA: Strutting like an ageing majorette, are we?

MIKE: I'm going to have to dash. I will see you later.

MIRANDA: OK.

They kiss.

MIKE: I love you.

MIRANDA: (FANS) Oh! Well, um… (HUMS THE NOKIA THEME TUNE AND PICKS UP HER FORK) Hello?

Gary switches on the power tool at mains. It shudders on the bar. He screams. Mike picks it up and switches it off.

GARY
VS
MIKE

GARY: (TAKING POWER TOOL) Thank you, Mike. I don't need a man who cries about a dog to show me how to—

MIKE: Actually Daisy's been with us for fifteen years.

GARY: How do you turn this on?

Mike switches it back on, revs it. Gary revs it back. **BOYS!**

MIRANDA: (TO CAMERA) It's not just me that's finding this erotic is it? (TO THEM) Keep wielding, men!

They stare. Miranda clocks camera.

INT. SHOP

Miranda gallops in. Stevie is working and still cross.

MIRANDA: Stevie, Stevie, Stevie, Stevie, Stevie... Mike just told me he loved me again and I couldn't reply.

STEVIE: Talk to the face 'cos the hand ain't listening!

MIRANDA & STEVIE: That's the wrong way round.

MIRANDA: Yeah. Oh, come on Stevie I need you. We're like a sofa and a little pouffe. It's clean sheet night tonight. Who am I going to change my duvet with? We could play 'Sheet Over Head Guess What Fruit's Being Thrown at You?' You love that!   😐 GORDON

Penny enters, on the phone.

265

PENNY: Delicious to talk to you darling, lots of love, bye! (PRESSES BUTTON ON PHONE) Ghastly woman.

BELINDA: (OOV – FROM PHONE) Who is?

MIRANDA: (WHISPERS) You're still on speaker. She's still there, she's still there.

PENNY: (JUMPS; COVERING UP) Ghastly woman I see before me… yes, Miranda. (FAKE LAUGH) Bye Belinda. (MIRANDA SWITCHES PHONE OFF) She's convinced that my tennis dinner won't be nearly as good as hers last year. Over my yoga-plated, flab free, super firm, what I call, buttocks. Now, do you think that Mike would…

Suddenly Raymond Blanc walks in. Penny does a double take and starts whispering and pointing excitedly. Stevie does the same.

MIRANDA: (TO CAMERA) What's happening? (SEES HIM) Oh, oh. Raymond Blanc! (TO PENNY AND STEVIE) You look like you're doing Riverdance.

PENNY: You'd be the same if your pin-up suddenly walked in.

STEVIE: Is Gary Barlow here?

MIRANDA: Is Theo Paphitis here?

STEVIE & PENNY: Theo Paphitis?

Makes no sense but funny!

Miranda clocks camera.

PENNY: (GASPS) I could ask Raymond to the dinner. If I got a celeb to the do – in your face, Belinda!

Penny approaches Raymond.

PENNY: Bonjour Monsieur Blanc.

RAYMOND: Bonjour mademoiselle.

PENNY: (LAUGHS COQUETTISHLY) Je suis avoir un soiree. Je voudrais vous... tu? Sorry, spat... (SHE WIPES HIS FACE) Pour le mingling. And I can give you a good function. No, no, no, I don't mean... unless... (FRENCH NOISES) Pardon!

Tell Patricia it's like she has turned into Miranda at this point

Raymond starts to leave.

PENNY: He's going. (FOLLOWS)

MIRANDA: Don't start stalking again.

PENNY: I'll observe with binoculars at the minimum distance as laid down by Barry Mannilow's lawyers.

She exits.

MIRANDA: (TO STEVIE) I presume you're still not speaking to me. So as your superior I would like you to send off this letter to British Gas. Thanking you.

Pointing at it on counter. She goes upstairs and trips.

STEVIE: Tripped.

MIRANDA: I meant to. I meant to go up the stairs like this.

She trips and skips the whole way up.

Fade to black.

INT. MIRANDA'S SITTING ROOM

Miranda starts to change duvet cover.

MIRANDA: Right OK, I can change a duvet cover on my own. Don't need her help, it's fine.

She gets in a complete muddle by doing the turning cover inside out and release manoeuvre, but she has the wrong corners, she ends up inside the duvet trying to crossly work it out.

MIRANDA: Stevie! I can't find the right corners!

INT. SHOP

Miranda comes down the stairs.

MIRANDA: Stevie. Be my friend again. If somebody's pulling a duvet cover on, (SINGS) she's the one.

JIM: (SINGS TO HIMSELF) She's the one-one-one.

Miranda looks to him and to camera, unnerved. Mike rushes in.

MIKE: (TO MIRANDA) Wallet, wallet, wallet, where, where, where, where?

We must make sure we never know his name. M & Stevie shouldn't call him anything. Funnier.

MIRANDA: Table, table, table. Everyone's at odds, odds, odds!

He goes upstairs.

Seriously now Stevie, what happens if he says I love you again? OK this is code red. Amber alert rising to pink, dogger moving east, showers later. That's the shipping forecast! (TO JIM) You, how do I tell someone I love them?

JIM: Oh um write it on a muffin and give it to him.

Note to self: be physically v panicked – turning on heels etc. Jittery

MIRANDA: Well even if I knew how to make a muffin I wouldn't have time to make a muffin, he's upstairs!

JIM: I didn't know that.

MIRANDA: Think!

Mike comes running downstairs.

MIKE: Sorry I shouted. Crazy day. Um, I'm no, I'll tell you later. I love you.

MIRANDA: Well I, err, I... Eyes are (A DITTY) to see with, noses are to smell with.

Mike smiles and exits. Jim is looking bewildered. He has his back to Miranda and Mike.

He mustn't see Mike for Later. Help these are complex sequences.

MIRANDA: (TO JIM) That was your fault. Now help me workshop why I can't say I love you. Stay and hang.

JIM: No, I should really—

MIRANDA: STAY AND HANG!

JIM: Right, well, what springs to mind when I say, what do you love?

MIRANDA: Good, liking this. Don't worry, Stevie, I've got a new friend.

Stevie angry marches to the kitchen.

Strutting like a toddler modelling Baby Gap, are we? (TO JIM) Right.

JIM: OK, what do you love?

MIRANDA: Doughnuts.

JIM: Again, what was your first love?

MIRANDA: Doughnuts.

JIM: More emotional. What makes your heart skip?

MIRANDA: Doughnuts.

JIM: I think I know what this means. You're not in love your boyfriend and it's only fair to split up with him.

He starts to go.

MIRANDA: (PANICKING) What? What? You can't leave me with that! Oh, my lovely Mike. I'm going to beanbag.

She collapses on bean bag, panicking.

Stevie. Stevie!

STEVIE: Miranda?

MIRANDA: He said... (HIGH PITCHED PANIC)

STEVIE: Alright, calm. (TO JIM) Now step back, I'm Miranda's number one workshopper. She's emotionally constipated and I'm her metaphorical prune.

MIRANDA: She's back. Love oo!

STEVIE: Luv oo.

They hug.

JIM: Love oo!

He goes to hug them

MIRANDA & STEVIE: No!

STEVIE: Now... (HELPS MIRANDA OUT OF BEAN BAG). As (POINTING AT JIM) this suggests, Mike is not what makes your heart skip. I mean you love him but you're not in love with him. That's why you can't say it. I'm right aren't I?

MIRANDA: Yes. Oh my Marple!

will people remember the nicknames Marple and Quirky. Bit naff

STEVIE: Now, we need to work out how you'll end it.

JIM: Can't she just tell him?

STEVIE: Just tell him? This guy! Miranda can't be direct. It's a condition. I call it Pushy Mother-itis and Acute English-ness-ness-ness. She had to write a letter to switch gas suppliers.

MIRANDA: Too scared to ring. They make me feel guilty, I end up signed to all protection plans and offering them a place to stay if they ever visit from Mumbai. I mean to be fair, Raj and Miri were very nice.

STEVIE: Oh they were lovely.

MIRANDA: I'm gonna have to write Mike a letter, it's the only way.

JIM & STEVIE: It's too mean!

STEVIE: Come on. Think and pace.

JIM: No, I really should be going.

should farcically do same movement. Might have to ask actors to stay late for this ep rehearsal wise.

STEVIE: Think and pace!

Miranda and Stevie pace. Jim starts to copy.

KEEP CALM

INT. SHOP – A LITTLE LATER

There is a flip chart up with 'How To Dump' as a heading.

A list of suggestions include: dumpogram, get Stevie to do it, text, email, interpretive dance…

STEVIE: Well we've run out of options.

MIRANDA: Well I've written him that letter…

STEVIE: You can't send that. Why can't you be less mimsy?

Penny enters with binoculars around her neck.

PENNY: What's going on?

JIM: She can't be direct because of a pushy mother…

Miranda and Stevie run forward in panic.

STEVIE: …She loves very much.

MIRANDA: (TO JIM) That's my mother.

JIM: Oh heavens above!

PENNY: Who is this?

MIRANDA & STEVIE: We don't know.

PENNY: I'm not pushy. Now Miranda, you are to drop everything and order Mike to help me tonight. I can't find Raymond but Mike could get us news coverage for the dinner.

JIM: (LOOKING OUT) Isn't that Raymond Blanc?

PENNY: Where? Where?

She rushes out, bumps into Mike and pushes him to one side.

Oh get out of the way!

Seeing Mike, Stevie pushes the flipchart over.

MIKE: What's going on?

Why he can't see Mike earlier.

JIM: We're workshopping because she realises she doesn't love Mike.

MIRANDA: Mike Owen. Mike Owen. Mark Owen. I don't love Mark Owen.

STEVIE: Nor do I. I love Gary Barlow.

Jim looks confused.

MIRANDA: (WHISPERING TO JIM) That's Mike.

JIM: This is a nightmare!

MIRANDA: (TO MIKE) She loves Gary Barlow.

JIM: I love Mark Owen.

MIRANDA: He loves Mark Owen. I love Robbie Williams.

JIM: We're setting up a Take That tribute band.

REHEARSE REHEARSE REHEARSE

ALL: (SINGING) Never forget, where you're coming from.

JIM: (OVER-THE-TOP SINGING) Never pretend that it's all real.

MIRANDA: (TO JIM) Too much.

MIKE: Right. I forgot I need a tie. I left one here. And we need to have a talk at some point.

He goes upstairs.

JIM: Ah, but what does he need to talk about? If I'm not mistaken he's got proposey eyes.

STEVIE: Don't be ridiculous, she's splitting up with him.

MIRANDA: Oh but I'm still mimsy. The thought of telling him, he's so gorgeous.

We hear a door slam. Stevie and Jim hide behind the counter. Mike comes down.

MIRANDA: And the thing is well now it looks like I'm talking to no one! Mike, listen, I need to talk to you actually. I love being with you but I just feel that I need a breather. Breeder. Breeder. Dog breeder. Horses. Horse dogs. I'm gonna breed horse dogs. Yeah. Dogs that you can ride. Dog dressage. Neigh! Woof! Sorry, I'm all over the place like soap in a shower. (BOUNCES UP AND DOWN) Where is it? Where's the soap? Where has it gone? (GRABS HER LETTER) Right OK, hang on, it says it all there.

Mike reads the letter.

MIKE: OK, well, it's a bold decision but I understand.

MIRANDA: You do?

MIKE: Yeah, if you want to leave British Gas it's your call.

MIRANDA: Wrong letter! (TO CAMERA) Wrong letter!

JIM & STEVIE: Wrong letter! Wrong letter!

FARCE PACE.

Miranda spins in a panic.

STEVIE: Follow him! Emergency walk! Go!

Miranda emergency walks out.

EXT. STREET

Mike is ahead tying his tie. Miranda emergency walking.

MIRANDA: Mike. Mike. Hi, listen. You know you were talking about working abroad? Well maybe that's a good idea.

MIKE: Oh my.

MIRANDA: I'm so sorry.

MIKE: It's Raymond Blanc. I'm a massive fan. (TO RAYMOND) My name's Michael Jackford. I work at the television station.

Mike shakes his hand and starts to walk with him. Miranda looks annoyed. We see Penny on the other side of the road with binoculars stalking Raymond. She doesn't look where she is going and falls into a road sweeper's bin.

Patricia or stunt double?

INT. SHOP

Miranda, Stevie and Jim are sitting with cups of tea.

MIRANDA: Today was meant to be a good day, it had a frisson about it.

Stevie with a massive mug as Sarah will LOVE THAT!

Stevie takes her cup to the kitchen.

JIM: I should go. I don't even know why I'm still here.

Jim takes his cup to the kitchen. Gary rushes in. Tea towel over his shoulder. Power tool in belt.

GARY: Hi.

MIRANDA: Oh, are you OK?

GARY: Stressed! Cooking deliveries. Rose keeps texting – even though we're not together she still wants to come tonight. Listen, I really, really need your help. Do you think you could spare a few hours this afternoon?

MIRANDA: Yeah, sure, I'll come over later.

GARY: Oh, thank you, thank you. (KISSES HER & EXITS) Oh! And by the way, man has put up sign. (WHIRS POWER TOOL; SCREAMS) Don't laugh.

HE GOES. STEVIE ENTERS.

MIRANDA: I wouldn't laugh. It's one of the reasons I love you.

STEVIE: What did you just say?

MIRANDA: I just said I love you but I mean, just flippantly. How I say it to you.

STEVIE: Well that's where you're mistaken my massive friend. We say it in a silly way. Look, tell me you love me.

MIRANDA: Love oo. (REALISES)

STEVIE: Please say you're finally getting this. What truly makes your heart skip?

MIRANDA: Gary.

STEVIE: How do you see Mike?

INT. FLAT (FANTASY)

Miranda is sitting on the sofa. Mike comes over with two cups of tea. Both are wearing dressing gowns.

MIKE: There we go.

Mike kisses her forehead.

MUSIC OUT

MUSIC IN

'Relax'

By Frankie Goes to Hollywood

INT. SHOP

STEVIE: How do you see Gary?

INT. FLAT (FANTASY)

Miranda is sitting on the sofa.

Gary comes over in army bottoms, topless, like Rambo. Jumps onto the sofa and kisses her passionately.

INT. SHOP

STEVIE: Who do you love?

MIRANDA: Gary. I'm in love with Gary!

STEVIE: Yes! I've been waiting three years for this.

They jump up and down. Jim enters from the kitchen.

She said I love you.

JIM: To who?

Big passionate reveal – audience should be v. happy.

MIRANDA: Gary. I love Gary. (TO CAMERA) I'm in love with Gary.

JIM: Who's Gary?

MIRANDA & STEVIE: (SINGING) I'm on the top of the world, looking down on creation…

JIM: Who's Gary?

Dance too.
KEEP UP
ENERGY

MIRANDA & STEVIE: (SINGING) And the only explanation I can find…

JIM: (SHOUTS) I demand to know who Gary is!

MIRANDA: He's an old friend from uni.

STEVIE: She's always loved him.

MIRANDA: I want to tell him. Do you think he feels the same?

STEVIE: Of course he feels the same. The minute Mike told you he loved you I clocked Gary's face.

STEVIE & MIRANDA: (SINGING) And the love that I've found…

JIM: (SHOUTS) But wait, wait! You have to split up with Mike before you tell Gary.

MIRANDA: Oh, how?

STEVIE: Focus. Knock out your mimsy.

MIRANDA: Hope that's not a euphemism.

STEVIE: Concentrate! Love is at stake.

JIM: This is serious now!

INT. MIRANDA'S SITTING ROOM

Miranda is pacing.

MIRANDA: I am a direct woman. I am soft, strong and very very long, no that's loo paper.

Mike knocks at the open door and enters.

MIKE: Hi, I got your text.

MIRANDA: Great, listen I need to speak to you.

She ushers him to the sofa.

Um, OK. Right, here is the thing, Mike. You are an amazing man and a wonderful boyfriend but I have to end—

Mike gets a text.

MIKE: Oh! Sorry. (LOOKS AT THE MESSAGE)
Oh it's Dad. Oh no! Daisy's gone. Oh! Sorry I know she's only a dog but I'm gonna have to go. Sorry, what were you saying?

MIRANDA: Oh, it's not important now.

MIKE: Something about having to end.

MIRANDA: Having to end a contract with BT and move to a new broadband package.

MIKE: That's what you wanted to tell me.

MIRANDA: (DRAMATICALLY) It's been very difficult, Mike.

Mike exits.

(TO CAMERA) This is getting out of control. I'm having to act!

HA.

INT. SHOP

Miranda and Mike walk down the stairs to the door.

STEVIE: Aahh, Mike, she's told you.

MIRANDA: About me moving to a new broadband package.
(NODDING AT STEVIE)

Keep energy going. It shouldn't really ever drop.

STEVIE: Oh yes, yes, tough times.

MIRANDA: Mike's upset because his dog just died just now.

JIM: Oh that is so annoying. Typical. Isn't that annoying?

MIKE: Who's this?

MIRANDA & STEVIE: We don't know.

Mike exits.

MIRANDA: I thought I was about to say it. I'm ready to explode like an emotional balloon.

STEVIE: Calm, you don't need to tell Gary now. The only reason to panic was if Rose was getting her claws in.

MIRANDA: She's been texting!

STEVIE: He's not interested so wait till Mike feels better.

JIM: Who's Rose?

Gary enters.

GARY: Is everything all right?

JIM: She's an emotional balloon because she's in love with Gary.

MIRANDA: Gary Barlow. (POINTS AT STEVIE) She loves Gary Barlow.

STEVIE: I love Gary Barlow.

MIRANDA: (WHISPERS TO JIM) That's Gary.

JIM: Why does it keep happening?

STEVIE: She loves Robbie Williams.

JIM: I love Mark Owen. We're a Take That tribute band.

ALL: (SINGING) Relight my fire.

JIM: (OVER THE TOP) Your love is my only desi...

Miranda & Stevie stare. He stops.

GARY: Lovely, Miranda just a quick one.

MIRANDA: Yes please! ——— *Too carry on?!*

GARY: I thought you were coming to help? But clearly you didn't mean it, so do you know what? Don't bother, Rose is coming.

Miranda and Stevie and Jim scream. Gary screams and gets on a chair.

What?

He realises he's embarrassed himself and exits.

MIRANDA: I couldn't love him more. Stupid Rose!

JIM: (SHOUTING ANGRILY) Now, I demand to know who Rose is.

STEVIE & MIRANDA: Gary's ex. Keep up!

STEVIE: Well you have to tell Gary now. Rose can't get there first. You can't miss the one thing that makes you happiest in the world. If I had a chance with my Gary I'd have (SINGING) One night, one night in heaven...

MIRANDA: Oh, well. You have done yourself proud with this.

good old Hadders & Heather

STEVIE: I know.

MIRANDA: OK, I'm gonna tell him. Febreeze me out.

Stevie squirts Febreeze. Miranda walks through it. She turns with crossed fingers. Jim and Stevie cross fingers too.

INT. RESTAURANT

Gary is behind the bar. Miranda walks in.

GARY: (NOT LOOKING UP) Oh we're not open till seven, sorry.

MIRANDA: It's me.

GARY: (ANNOYED) Oh, hi.

MIRANDA: Hi. Listen, I'm so sorry I let you down earlier but by way of an apology I want to tell you that well Gary, I know I've being seeing Mike but I realise now that (TAKES A BREATH). Gary Preston...

GARY: Oh my, Miranda, I don't believe it.

MIRANDA: Well let me say it.

GARY: It's Raymond Blanc!

Miranda turns around.

MIRANDA: (IN HIS FACE) Raymond bloody Blanc! I'll Michel Roux the day I met you! (TO CAMERA) Oh! That was quite clever wasn't it? You keep messing up my life.

RAYMOND: And I am hiding from that crazy woman.

GARY: Mr Blanc, Mr Blanc, hello, um sorry a bit star struck, err it's actually my restaurant opening tonight, do you think you might be able to come?

RAYMOND: Actually I'm looking for a restaurant to meet a friend tonight.

GARY: Amazing!

We see Penny in the coat stand.

PENNY: Non, non, non!

Miranda screams.

Penny shuffles forward with coat stand attached.

Raymond! Come to mon tennis dinner.

Poor Patricia Hodge!

MIRANDA: I have no idea who this woman is.
(TO PENNY) Such fun.

She exits.

INT. SHOP

Bloody too rude?
8.30 BBC 1.

JIM, STEVIE & MIRANDA: Ray ruddy White!

MIRANDA: I have to get in there before Rose.

STEVIE: She romances Gary. She gets him with sweeping gestures.

STEVIE & MIRANDA: Think.

JIM: Ooh, you've got to out - Rose Rose.

STEVIE: Oh, yes! Romance is my area. I'm thinking picnic, champers, doves. Such is my allure, I naturally woo with every sense. The smell of my skin, the touch of my clothes, the sight of my cleavage.

MIRANDA: Excuse me I am the woo-er here.

287

STEVIE: Well I thought you were desperate for my help but do go on.

MIRANDA: Fine, I will. I can do this, I can woo with my every sense. The touch of my clothes, the, what was it? The smell of my underwear, the sound of my cleavage. OK, that's wrong. You do it!

STEVIE: Meet Gary in the park in two hours.

JIM: This is the best day of my life!

MIRANDA: (TO CAMERA) Bit weird.

EXT. PARK

Miranda has changed. She is sitting on a picnic rug. There is an ice bucket with champagne. Rose petals etc. She is trying to sit elegantly.

MIRANDA: When did it get so hard to sit on the floor? *SO TRUE AGEING.....*

She tries sitting cross-legged. Gary approaches.

MIRANDA: Hi!

She attempts a sexy lying position.

GARY: What's all this? I thought I was meeting Stevie.

MIRANDA: It's a gesture. From me. Not Stevie.

GARY: Well that's very kind but I'm really busy.

MIRANDA: No Gary, wait, wait. I thought you might need a break and I wanted to say I'm so sorry about not helping.
(HANDS HIM CHAMPAGNE)

GARY: OK. Alright. Thank you.

They sit.

Can you hear music?

Miranda looks confused. She looks up and sees Jim up the tree with a CD player.

MIRANDA: No. No. No, look, um, look down. Look at this cream!

GARY: What? I don't want to look at —

MIRANDA: Really closely, Gary.

Miranda pushes the tub of strawberries and cream too close so his face goes in.

Oh sorry. Sorry. Sorry, cream nose.

A moment. Suddenly white geese appear.

GARY: Where did the geese come from?

Miranda looks around and sees Stevie in a bush doing thumbs up.

Help.

Miranda and Gary stand up. The geese come closer. Gary runs. Miranda chases after him. Then a goose chases her.

MIRANDA: Ooh, they are scary. Stevie?

STEVIE: (CHASING MIRANDA AND GARY) I couldn't get doves!

Gary hides behind a bush, as does Miranda.

GARY: Is this your idea of a joke?

MIRANDA: They've gone.

They come out of the bush.

They're back!

The geese chase them all. HOW ON EARTH?!

STEVIE: Ooh, they are scary!

ALL: It's the hissing!

INT. RESTAURANT

Gary enters, then Miranda. Then Stevie with the ice bucket and champers, then Jim with CD player.

MIRANDA: I was trying to say something.

GARY: Oh Miranda, only you. Just tell me.

MIRANDA: OK. Oh I can't look at you!

GARY: What? Oh, this is important isn't it? Just let me just get this cream from out of my nose.

Goes to kitchen. Close up of Miranda closing her eyes. NEED TO BELIEVE
Then we see a pair of hands cover her eyes. THEY ARE GARY'S
HANDS

MIRANDA: Hi. OK, listen. Here's the thing. And I'm sorry I've been going about it in such a roundabout way particularly as I've never been so certain of anything in my life. I am absolutely, ridiculously, embarrassingly in love with you.

Miranda turns around and we pull back to reveal it was Mike. Who is beaming. Miranda screams. Turns scream to excitement.

Oh! Mike.

Stevie and Jim scream, knock over the ice bucket and turn screams in to joy.

MIKE: And I was just going to say, guess who?

Gary comes in from kitchen.

GARY: (TO MIRANDA) OK, what is it?

MIRANDA: Moment's gone!

MIKE: I've been waiting to hear that.

MIRANDA: Well it was lucky you were here then. Why were you here then?

Penny enters.

PENNY: Oh, Mike, now, about my dinner—

MIRANDA: (FURIOUSLY) Oh, Mother!

MIKE: Penny, there's something I need to ask Miranda's father.

JIM: (SHRIEKS) Proposey eyes!

He jumps and tips table over.

GARY: Oh, table! I've just laid that!

PENNY: He wants to speak to your father. Oh darling!

Mike and Penny exit. Rose arrives.

STEVIE: Oh no! It's Rose.

MIRANDA: Do something.

Stevie grabs Gary and snogs him.

They need to linger. Height difference issue for snogging?!!!

MIRANDA: (TO CAMERA) How does that help?

ROSE: Well I'm clearly in the way, I didn't realise you two were—

STEVIE: Yeah. So, you know, bye.

GARY: Rose, wait, I don't even know why she kissed me.

ROSE: Well it looked pretty passionate to me, you lingered.

MIRANDA: Agreed m'lord there was lingering.

JIM: I thought there was lingering.

ROSE: Who are you?

JIM: I don't know.

MIRANDA & ROSE: You both lingered.

GARY & STEVIE: We did not linger.

Miranda and Rose start to leave.

GARY: Rose!

STEVIE: Miranda!

They put their hands up as if to say 'not listening'.

MIRANDA: Sweeping out. (SHE SLIPS) Oh, ice! You know when you nearly go? I nearly went. (SHE SLIPS AGAIN, THEN FALLS) Oh, I've gone!

INT. FLAT

Jim inbetween Miranda and Stevie on the sofa.

MIRANDA: You kissed my Gary. How would you like it if I kissed yours? I'm going to get my own back and snog Gary Barlow, OK, that's never going to happen.

STEVIE: I was trying to get rid of her.

MIRANDA: Well you shouldn't have interfered.

STEVIE: Didn't want to but, 'Stevie, I can't cope we're a sofa and a little pouffe'—

MIRANDA: Oh, je me suis… (SHE STARTS SPEAKING IN PRETEND FRENCH–SUBTITLED)

SUBTITLE IN

I am so angry I am speaking in fake French.

She won't know it's fake French

And to save face will gasp

When I sound like I am being offensive.

SUBTITLE OUT

Stevie gasps. Miranda clocks camera.

(TO JIM) Right, you, whatever your name is, I bequeath you the status of my new best friend.

JIM: Oh, it's too much!

MIRANDA: Change the duvet with me please. Now.

Stevie goes. Penny rushes in. Pushing Stevie in.

PENNY: Darling, darling. Mike's just spoken to your father. He's going to propose. You will say yes?

JIM: No, she can't marry a man she doesn't really love.

STEVIE: What she needs is someone who knows her and gets her.

PENNY: What she needs is someone who doesn't know her and will only know what he's getting when it's too late!

MIRANDA: (TO CAMERA) Am I here? I think I'm here.

MIKE: (OOV) Miranda?

MIRANDA: Hide, hide, hide!

Jim goes to the bedroom. Penny and Stevie hide in front of the sofa. Mike enters. Miranda has nowhere to hide.

Hide. Hi. Hi-de-hi! *Jittery again. *PHYSICALISE**

MIKE: Hi, can we talk?

MIRANDA: Yeah sure um what would you like to talk about? I'm worried about the Greek economy. Discuss.

Mike and Miranda move to in front of the sofa. Penny and Stevie crawl round to the back of it.

Mike gets down on one knee. Penny and Stevie poke up and inhale sharply.

Miranda starts singing to cover up.

MIRANDA: What are you doing?

MIKE: Tying my shoe lace.

Stevie and Penny pop up.

STEVIE: Phew!

PENNY: Sugar!

They duck back down.

MIKE: What?

MIRANDA: Few sugars I shall make in your tea now for you. Yes. (POINTING) Is that a barn owl?

She ushers Penny and Stevie to the bathroom and throws the duvet cover over Mike.

MIKE: Just forget about the tea. Will you just sit for one moment? You're so skittish today.

MIRANDA: Like a little pony.

MIKE: So listen, I know we've only been seeing each other for a few weeks but I've been thinking about the future.

A knock on the door. It's a man in a uniform — trousers, jacket, cap.

BT MAN: Hi, can I speak to Miranda please?

MIRANDA: Yes.

BT MAN: Oh hi, I'm from BT.

MIRANDA: Hi.

BT MAN: I'm really sorry you're not happy at the moment.

MIRANDA: Oh listen, I did mean it.

Stevie and Penny open the bathroom door a tiny bit. They are straining to hear

MIRANDA: It's not you it's me, I just want to be with someone else. Bye.

She shuts the door. Penny and Stevie come out — they don't see Mike on the sofa.

STEVIE: Yay, mimsy-less!

PENNY: Disappointing!

MIKE: What are you doing here?

Penny and Stevie jump.

MIRANDA: They are here to wish me well, err, for letting go of BT.

Handwritten note: Have to make it believable they are just listening & not looking. can't see

Farce is a NIGHTMARE!

MIKE: So why were you in the bathroom?

PENNY: We urgently needed the loo. We didn't go together.

STEVIE: I went first.

PENNY: I followed through. *SILLY.*

MIRANDA: OK. Bye then guys. Thanks so much for coming.

Penny and Stevie leave.

MIKE: Look, I don't know what's going on here but will you just listen to me before I burst?

MIRANDA: Wait, Mike listen, I'm in love with—

MIKE: I've taken a job in Africa.

MIRANDA: What?

MIKE: But I mean, after what you said at the restaurant, just say if you don't want me to go.

MIRANDA: Oh no, you must go, it's what you've always wanted.

MIKE: What were you...? You're in love with?

MIRANDA: In love with... Talk Talk for my new ISP.

MIKE: I have never known a family so emotional about service providers.

MIRANDA: Oh, I'll miss you, Marple.

MIKE: Oh, I'll miss you so much, Quirky, but let's talk, yeah?

They kiss and hug.

MIRANDA: Yeah. Bye.

MIKE: Bye.

He exits. She goes to the sofa and pulls the duvet over her head.

MIRANDA: Alone again.

Jim pops out from under the duvet.

JIM: You've got me!

Miranda screams.

INT. RESTAURANT

It's the opening. Tea lights. Fairy lights. The shelf is back up. People at tables. Some milling. There is a kind of buffet system. The food coming from outside waiters bringing it in.

Miranda is sitting at one table with food. Stevie comes over from the buffet with a plate of food. Walks past and sits at another table. Penny comes in.

MIRANDA: Why aren't you at the tennis club?

PENNY: One glimpse of Belinda's smug face that it was a celeb-and-press free mediocre event and I abandoned.

Raymond Blanc enters.

GARY: Oh Raymond's here! Evening Mr Blanc, thank you for coming. (FAKE FRENCH ACCENT) Your table is over here.

MIRANDA: Pretend you're enjoying yourself for Gary.

They fake laugh.

GARY: What are you doing?

MIRANDA: We're creating ambience.

They fake laugh again.

GARY: Can you just stay out of it please?

MIRANDA: Why are you so angry with me?

GARY: Shush, Raymond is behind you.

MIRANDA: I don't care about Raymond. He ruined my day.

GARY: And you ruined mine. The one day I needed your help.

MIRANDA: Well maybe I had urgent things to do.

GARY: What, like rehearse a Take That tribute band?

He goes off, but comes back angrily.

You know, there's always something with you isn't there? Hey, on the one day I was struggling and needed your help, like you always do, your issues are still more important – although they very rarely are.

MIRANDA: They *were* more important!

GARY: (REALLY ANGRY) Oh, what? What was more important?

MIRANDA: (SHOUTS) Splitting up with my boyfriend and telling you I'm completely and utterly head over heels in love with you. I love you!

Rose walks in. Gary is stunned. The restaurant goes silent. Rose walks out.

PENNY: Oh that's embarrassing. (TO MIRANDA) Do something more embarrassing so it won't seem so embarrassing.

MIRANDA: (SINGING) I'm a little coconut, ugly and hairy, but when you crack me open I ooze milk and nut.

no idea where this came from! Hope not too surreal for audience. I like.

PENNY: No, that's worse. (LOUDLY) I have no idea who this woman is.

She exits.

MIRANDA: Right, I'm just gonna flush myself down a plug hole.

Penny comes back in.

PENNY: You'll never guess who's here to meet Raymond.

oh they will be.

Penny leads in Gary Barlow. Everyone is amazed.

Mr Gary Barlow, would you make an appearance at my tennis club dinner?

GARY BARLOW: For you, anything.

He kisses her hand.

PENNY: Take that Blanc, we've got Barlow.

MIRANDA: Mr Gary Barlow.

Miranda takes him by the hand and kisses him in front of Stevie.

(TO STEVIE) I lingered.
(TO CAMERA) Yes! THIS IS GOING TO BE SURREAL

INT. FLAT

Miranda is sitting on the sofa. The telly is on. It's karaoke.

MIRANDA: He didn't say it back, he could have said it back.

STEVIE: You've got me.

MIRANDA & STEVIE: Love oo.

JIM: And me. And our band. Take That's on karaoke.

Miranda puts volume up. It's "Back For Good".
They pick up mics.

MIRANDA, STEVIE & JIM: (SINGING) Whatever I said, whatever I did, I didn't mean it. I just want you back for good. Want you back. I want you back. I want you back for good.

Caption

You have been watching

Miranda Hart
Sarah Hadland
Dominic Coleman
Tom Ellis
Bo Poraj
Naomi Bentley
Raymond Blanc
Patricia Hodge
Gary Barlow

INT. FLAT

Miranda, Jim and Stevie are still all singing along to the music.
Jim hugging Miranda.

MIRANDA: (TO JIM) You will have to leave at some point.

The rest of the cast join in and sing along with the music.

Fade to black

Series Three, Episode Five:
Behind the Scenes Tit-Bits

There was a slightly awkward moment when on the day of the record I had to ask Gary Barlow if he wanted to rehearse the kiss. The answer was a resounding no!

All the cast are huge Take That fans and singing 'Back For Good' with Gary for the end sequence, well, I don't think you have seen us happier. We have all now put on our CVs 'toured with Take That'.

We had to keep Gary's presence a secret from the studio audience and so we gave him a code name. Aubergine. I have no idea where that came from.

Don't work with geese unless you really have to! They are totally uncontrollable. It was utter chaos trying to get them to run in the right direction to chase us.

Two words: Raymond Blanc. He is as charming as you can imagine although I think was a little frightened by the crazy women around him.

What a sport. I'll always feel bad for shouting at him with the line 'I shall Michel Roux the day I ever met you.' I never did it fully in rehearsal and he got a bit of a shock on the night.

In many ways, as a writer I felt like the show was kind of starting now. Gary is putting down roots and buying the restaurant. All the characters feel very grounded in who they are. Miranda has grown into herself and isn't *quite* such a heightened clown. I know exactly what the actors like and don't like and how to best serve their characters. Miranda and Stevie's relationship is nailed – they can fall out and compete but they always love each other. Deeply sisterly relationship. Having done the therapist episode in Series Two I felt I understood Miranda and Penny's complex mother–daughter relationship. So I felt I really had my sitcom at this point. It's just a shame that I was feeling pretty burnt out at the thought of going straight in to a fourth series. Leave on a high or push on. Always a tricky one. We'll see…

STEVIE'S CORNER

WELCOME TO THE ALLURE-OSPHERE

This week Stevie talks about having what she calls 'the allure', and why she thinks Miranda ONLY has 'wiles'.

'THE ALLURE'

noun

the quality of being powerfully and mysteriously attractive or fascinating.
'people for whom gold holds no allure'

People often approach me asking general questions about what it's like to have the allure so I thought I'd dedicate this page to it. I wasn't born with the 'allure', I earned it. I'm a self starter, I'm ambitious and I'm organised, giving me a huge head start when it comes to projecting the allure. People with the allure can sense the allure and only we know if other people have the allure. It's pretty straight forward really.

Sometimes people confuse the allure with 'wiles' but they're two completely different things. If you're not sure what you have, the only way to find out for the first time is to ask someone who has it like me. Because I am basically Captain of the Allure Society and everything within the allure-osphere.

'WILES'

noun

plural noun: wiles
Devious or cunning stratagems employed in manipulating or persuading someone to do what one wants.
'She had been trying out her feminine wiles on Gary'

Now I'm not being rude, but this is exactly what Miranda has. The allure and wiles can be easily confused. Don't fall into the same trap Miranda has. And FYI the allure is way better than even a thousand wiles. Fact.

KNOW THE SHOW?

How well do you...

1 Which life sized animal has its place in the Joke Shop?

2 What song was playing when Miranda's trousers fell down at a party?

3 What number is on Miranda's front door?

4 What was the name of the kitten in Miranda's suitcase at the airport?

5 Which episode did the fruit friends first appear?

Penny likes to call the remote control a ...? **6**

7 What does Miranda first catch whilst playing snack fishing?

What day did Miranda want her Christmas gift redelivered? **8**

9 What was the Wallet Guy's real name?

Who is taller, Penny or Stevie? **10**

You Have Been Reading . . .

Miranda: Miranda Hart
Stevie: Sarah Hadland
Penny: Patricia Hodge
Gary: Tom Ellis
Tilly: Sally Phillips
Clive: James Holmes
Mike: Bo Poraj
Rose: Naomi Bentley
Chris: John Finnemore
Alison: Margaret Cabourn-Smith

Valerie: Tim Pigott-Smith
Jim: Dominic Coleman
Therapist: Mark Heap
Tamara: Stacy Liu
Stinky: Belinda Stewart-Wilson

Director: Juliet May
Producer (Series 1): Nerys Evans
Producer (Series 2-3): Emma Strain
Exec Producer: Jo Sargent
Exec Producer (Series 2): Mark Freeland

Acknowledgements

Thank you very much, as ever, to Hannah Black and all the hard-working team at Hodder. And to my marvellous agent, Gordon Wise at Curtis Brown. (Gordon the Grapefruit in Series Two was for him!)

But my greatest thanks has to go to all the cast and crew on the sitcom. Every department was challenged on every episode in one way or another and they never failed to work hard to make the scripts work.

Particular reference to director Juliet May, floor manager Julia Sykes, all the cast, editor Jake and the amazing props guys and designer Harry Banks. Forever grateful, team.

And last but by no means least to Jo Sargent, who risked introducing me to the BBC. And to all those at the BBC for allowing me to put my vision on screen by expertly trusting and guiding, and not interfering: Jon Plowman, Lucy Lunsden, Cheryl Taylor, Mark Freeland, Roly Heating, Janice Hadlow. Thank you.

Publisher's Acknowledgements

The publishers would like to thank the cast members of Miranda for their kind permission to use their likeness in the images that appear in this book.

Cast List / Credits

Series One, Episode One: Date

Written by
Miranda Hart

Additional Material by
Paul Kerensa · Leisa Rea

Cast
Miranda: Miranda Hart · Penny: Patricia Hodge · Stevie: Sarah Hadland · Gary: Tom Ellis · Delivery Man: Ben Forster · Clive: James Holmes · Tilly: Sally Phillips · Fanny: Katy Wix · Vox Pop Woman (Woman 2): Helen Moon · Shop Assistant: Patrick Barlow · Paul (Camp Customer): Danny Edwards · Wedding Shop Assistant: Josie D'Arby

Series Two, Episode One: The New Me

Written by
Miranda Hart

with
Tony Roche · Georgia Pritchett · Paul Powell · James Cary · Richard Hurst · Paul Kerensa

Cast
Miranda: Miranda Hart · Stevie: Sarah Hadland · Posh Girl: Sophie Pelham · Tilly: Sally Phillips · Penny: Patricia Hodge · Stinky: Belinda Stewart-Wilson · Clive: James Holmes · Danny: Michael Landes · Life Coach: Mel Giedroyc · Ryan: Tom Parry · Bed Shop Customer: Vicki Hopps · Bed Shop Boss: John Voce · Michelle: Kerry Godliman · Gary:

Tom Ellis · PC Davis: James Doherty · Sandy: Karen Seacombe · Delivery Man: Ben Forster

Series Two, Episode Four: A New Low

Written by
Miranda Hart

with
Paul Kerensa · Paul Powell · Richard Hurst · James Cary

Cast
Miranda: Miranda Hart · Penny: Patricia Hodge · Tamara: Stacy Liu · Stevie: Sarah Hadland · Youth: Theo Barklem-Biggs · Clive: James Holmes · Builder: Andrew Thomas Jones · Gary: Tom Ellis · Helena: Anna Chancellor

Series Two, Episode Five: Just Act Normal

Written by
Miranda Hart

with
James Cary · Richard Hurst · Georgia Pritchett · Paul Kerensa · Paul Powell

Cast
Miranda: Miranda Hart · Penny: Patricia Hodge · Therapist: Mark Heap · Gary: Tom Ellis · PC Davis: James Doherty

Series Three, Episode Three: The Dinner Party

Written by
Miranda Hart

with
Richard Hurst · Georgia Pritchett · Paul Powell · Paul Kerensa

Cast
Miranda: Miranda Hart · Mike: Bo Poraj · Penny: Patricia Hodge · Yoga Instructor: Sarah Flower · Stevie: Sarah Hadland · Customer: Paul Kerensa · Plumber: Glen Davies · Alison: Margaret Cabourn-Smith · Gary: Tom Ellis · Rose: Naomi Bentley · Chris: John Finnemore · Childrens' Musical Playgroup Leader: Joanna Neary · Valerie: Tim Pigott-Smith · M&S Customer: Alice Hart · Traffic Warden: Joe Wilkinson

Series Three, Episode Five: Three Little words

Written by
Miranda Hart

with
Richard Hurst · Georgia Pritchett · Paul Powell · Paul Kerensa

Cast
Miranda: Miranda Hart · Mike: Bo Poraj · Penny: Patricia Hodge · Gary: Tom Ellis · Stevie: Sarah Hadland · Raymond Blanc: As himself · Customer (Jim): Dominic Coleman · Rose: Naomi Bentley · BT Man: Dan March · Gary Barlow: As himself

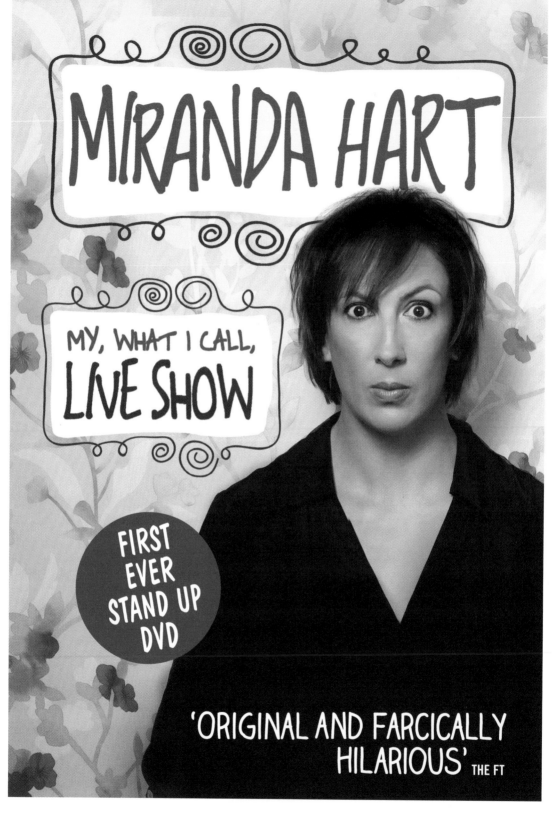

ORDER NOW ON DVD